# TERMS OF USE, DISCLAIMER AND COPYRIGHT

**Use of Brand Names and References:**
All trademarks, product names, or service names
mentioned in this book are the property of their respective
owners. Reference to any third-party content, research, or
tools is for illustrative or educational purposes and does
not imply sponsorship, endorsement, or affiliation.

**Academic Content Notice:**
Portions of this book draw from academic research,
including the author's dissertation.
All cited content is referenced in the bibliography in
accordance with academic standards.

**Publishing Imprint:**
Published by EP Publishing House
ISBN: 978-1-0492-0407-9 (print)
ISBN: 978-1-0492-1507-5 (electronic)
First Edition
Edited by An De Fortier
Printed and distributed in South Africa

No 22 Owl Rock road, Onrus, Hermanus, 7201
Contact Number: +27825666034
Email Address: estellepieterse21@gmail.com

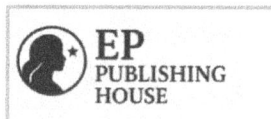

# Change your perspective, Change your Life!

## PREFACE

For much of my life, I've watched strong, capable women hesitate when it comes to financial planning—not because they lack intelligence, but because they've been left out of the conversation for too long. Cultural expectations, systemic barriers, and a lack of financial education have created a silent gap—one where too many women feel unsure, disempowered, or entirely disconnected from their own financial futures.

This book was born from a deep, personal conviction: **Financial independence is not optional—it's essential.** It's the key to freedom, dignity, and the ability to make choices, especially in times of crisis or transition.

With nearly three decades in the financial services industry—first as a young adviser and later as a business consultant, key individual, and franchise director—I've seen first-hand how powerful financial planning can be, especially for women. I've also conducted research into the unique barriers women face, and the insights are clear: progress is happening, but far too slowly. Many women still

3

don't feel confident managing their finances, and often they don't realise the risks of not doing so until it's too late.

You'll find the fundamentals of financial planning explained clearly and accessibly, along with tools to help you take action. But you'll also find stories—my own and others'—that remind us why this matters, and how financial literacy can transform not just bank accounts, but lives.

If you've ever felt overwhelmed, intimidated, or just unsure where to start, this book is for you.

Let's walk this path together.

By Estelle Pieterse

# TABLE OF CONTENTS

# ACKNOWLEDGEMENTS

Writing this book has been an enlightening and deeply personal journey. It led me to revisit many memories of the past—some painful, some powerful—to better understand where I find myself today. Along the way, I felt a deepened connection to God. In the quiet moments of reflection and prayer, I could clearly see His hand guiding me through daily challenges, offering wisdom when I asked, and sending the most beautiful rainbows as gentle reminders of His presence and promises.

To my brother and sister, who were deeply affected by decisions made by others—your strength and perseverance inspire me every single day. You have both risen above your circumstances to build lives and families filled with purpose and love. Your sheer resilience is a testimony to so many others that we do not have to be prisoners of our past—we have the power to shape our own future.

To every person who has come into my life, even for a season—thank you. Whether your role was small or significant, I have learned something from each encounter. These experiences have helped reinforce my passion for growth and transformation, and they fuel my desire to empower others to take ownership of their lives and financial journeys.

To my immediate family, and to everyone who has trusted, supported, and walked beside me—
thank you.

Thank you for the love, the laughter, the hard conversations, and the shared dreams. Thank you for a lifetime of memories and for making every day feel meaningful and special, even when we do not see each other regularly.

This book is for all of you.

# INTRODUCTION

Women's financial independence has come a long way, but **many still hesitate to take full control of their financial futures** and find themselves disconnected from their financial power. In a world where women are increasingly leading households, building careers, and outliving their male partners, the gap between opportunity and confidence in financial decision making is one we can no longer afford to ignore.

This book is designed to bridge that gap—**providing insights into financial planning, key legislative changes, and the evolving role of women in society**. By understanding and leveraging these advancements, women can confidently build a secure and independent financial future. **This book was written for the woman who**

- earns an income but feels unsure about planning for retirement.
- has relied on a partner to 'handle the money', but now wants to take control.
- is starting over after a loss, divorce, or career change.
- is young and ambitious but doesn't know where to begin with long-term planning.
- simply wants clarity in a space where financial advice often feels overwhelming or irrelevant.

Miles Kington, a British journalist, once humorously stated, **'Knowledge is knowing that a tomato is a fruit. Wisdom is not putting it in a fruit salad.'**

This quote perfectly illustrates a critical issue: **having access to information is not enough—understanding how to apply it is what truly matters.** The financial landscape, particularly related to legislation affecting women, has changed significantly in recent years. Yet, despite these opportunities, many women still lack the confidence to take control of their financial planning, relying instead on their male counterparts. This leaves them vulnerable—especially when unexpected life changes occur, such as divorce, widowhood, or career shifts. This book will

- **demystify** the essential principles of financial planning,
- **empower** you with knowledge and confidence to take charge of your finances, and
- **provide actionable steps** to create and implement a structured financial plan.

To illuminate women's attitudes towards financial planning, I have incorporated findings from my **2017 research study**, which explored the **barriers women face in managing their finances.** This book includes the **latest statistics** on financial trends and women's economic participation. It is concerning that **progress remains incremental.** Despite **legislative reforms creating opportunities,** many women **still do not fully leverage them,** even today!

This book is here to change that. It's time to move beyond hesitation and **embrace financial independence with confidence**. Financial independence is more than just having control over your finances; it's about building the life you want, overcoming challenges, and making empowered decisions. For me, this realisation came early in life, shaped not only by personal adversity and my mother's profound resilience but also by my Christian faith, which has been my anchor through every trial and triumph.

Let this be the beginning of a wiser, stronger, more secure future.

# PART I: FOUNDATIONS OF FINANCIAL EMPOWERMENT

## Chapter 1: A Personal Journey to Financial Empowerment

### 1.1 Early challenges and life experiences

Growing up, **my childhood was shaped by immense love, unwavering support, and high expectations**. My parents instilled strong **Christian values** in me from a young age, and these principles became my guiding light through both triumphs and trials. My father, the primary breadwinner, was a strict yet dedicated man who believed in the power of hard work. Having had limited opportunities himself and no formal qualifications, he was determined that his children would succeed through discipline and perseverance. As the eldest, I felt the weight of his expectations and the responsibility to excel.

Throughout my early years, my father was frequently called up for military service, often leaving for three-month stretches. These absences were difficult for our household, placing additional strain on my mother. Yet, it also reinforced my father's sense of duty and discipline, values he sought to instil in me and my younger siblings—a brother eight years my junior and a sister four years younger.

My parents married young, and neither had formal qualifications. Coming from large families—both were one of seven siblings—we were deeply connected to our extended relatives. My mother's family owned a well-established general store in Rustenburg, where all the nieces and nephews would 'work' during school holidays. It wasn't about earning money, but rather about spending time together, keeping our hands busy, and enjoying small rewards like Wilson toffees and Buddy Cokes. These early experiences, though playful, planted the first seeds of financial understanding and entrepreneurship in my young mind.

During my earliest years, my father was a farm manager for an international consortium outside Rustenburg, overseeing agricultural and game farming operations. Our family was tightly knit, and we visited my grandparents regularly, spending long, carefree days on their farm. My first two years of schooling were at a small primary school in Beestekraal, surrounded by vast open fields, where life felt simple and safe.

However, in 1980, everything changed. When the farms in the area were sold, we relocated to a plot outside Pretoria. My sister and I attended a small farm school with fewer than 100 children. The land was beautiful, and my father had plans to build our new dream home. He had ambitious goals and a strong work ethic, believing in paying for everything in cash and avoiding debt. At first, we lived in a modest tin house on the plot, and my father started construction on our dream home as finances allowed. But financial constraints meant that we lived in that temporary tin house for nearly seven years.

My father expected me especially, as the eldest, to excel in all areas—academics, sports, and leadership. Both my parents were actively involved in our school activities, always present on sports days and offering their assistance where needed. **My father was a proud and conservative man who firmly believed in a 'win or lose' philosophy— there was no in-between. It wasn't until much later in life that I realised success is not just about winning but about progress, resilience, and doing your best in the specific circumstances.** Still, his mindset shaped my own approach to life, driving me to push myself relentlessly. I thrived in school, eventually becoming head girl in primary school and earning the prestigious Victrix Ludorum award for excellence in sports.

However, the security of childhood was soon overshadowed by hardship.

During our time on the plot, my father was a director in a factory in Rosslyn, focusing on powder coating and sandblasting, alongside German business partners who provided capital for large projects. **His work demanded**

**long hours and social events, and he increasingly turned to alcohol as a coping mechanism.** The stress was evident. One vivid memory stands out—my father and his business partners, having secured a major contract, decided to celebrate by retreating to a game farm. They arrived at our home in a Volkswagen Combi to fetch my father, brimming with excitement, taking along 'entertainment' for the trip. Looking back, this moment encapsulated the societal norms and gender dynamics of the time, where indulgence and celebration were considered a privilege for men, while women were expected to **manage the home and family without question.**

But behind these moments of celebration, darker realities loomed. My father struggled with internal conflicts about the life he was building and the values he was betraying. As his moral battles intensified, so did the turmoil within our home. My mother became a victim of **gender-based violence**, feeling trapped by financial dependence and a deep sense of shame. Though she held onto her faith, praying for strength and wisdom, the incidents of violence grew more frequent.

As a teenager, I was deeply aware of the difference between right and wrong. I refused to look the other way. I held my father accountable, confronting him repeatedly. This inevitably strained our relationship, chipping away at the bond we once shared. **The cycle of violence was unbearable—we would leave, only to return after family**

**interventions and promises of change**. My mother, ever the forgiving wife, believed in second chances. I, on the other hand, was unwilling to accept empty apologies. The turning point came when my mother sustained serious injuries during an altercation. She refused medical attention, ashamed of the situation. We had left to stay with relatives, and I refused to go back home until my father sought professional help. A temporary separation was agreed upon, but the damage had already been done.

**At age 15, tragedy struck.** My father took his own life after we had returned to collect some personal belongings. The trauma of that incident is something I still carry with me. I've had to deal with the feeling of guilt for my part in the situation we were in, refusing to return before my dad had sought professional help, while my mom, longing to go back, tried to convince me after every conversation with him.

His **will was outdated, and financial policies and reviews were left incomplete** by a family friend and adviser. The bank account was frozen while there was a family feud, leaving my mother, my siblings, and me completely **financially and emotionally devastated**. His estate was bankrupt and was only wound up after 2 years. They were married in community of property, and we lost everything. Forced to permanently move in with relatives, my mother had no formal qualifications, no stable income, and no immediate way to rebuild our lives.

This was especially hard on my brother and sister.

With this sudden upheaval, I found myself navigating three different high schools, each transition marked by instability and uncertainty. **Survival became our priority.** My mother had to find a way to provide, despite the odds stacked against her. These experiences—of loss, resilience, and the power dynamics of financial dependence—became the foundation for my lifelong passion for **financial empowerment**.

## 1.2 Entrepreneurial beginnings and growth

My mother was a woman of **extraordinary resilience**. Despite never having received formal training, she taught herself how to draw house plans for prospective homeowners. For years, she worked on these plans while being a full-time housewife. This skill, which she had nurtured over time, became our lifeline after my father's passing.

With determination and faith, my mother transitioned into a formal position, where she qualified for a home loan subsidy. Through sheer perseverance, she built us a house from a plan she had drawn herself—a **tangible representation of God's provision**. Even in the most challenging times, we experienced acts of kindness from our neighbours would quietly leave bags of groceries on our doorstep when the month stretched too long.

Her ability to **rebuild from nothing** became the foundation of my own **entrepreneurial spirit**. Watching her navigate hardship with such grace and determination **inspired me to take charge of my own future**. The constant feeling of guilt over the situation that we found ourselves in was a key driver in every decision that I've made. Our home remained our *safe haven* for three years, but change was inevitable. My mother eventually remarried and **moved to another town with my younger brother**. My sister also left home, got married the following year, and started her own life. At this point, I knew I had to carve out my **own path,** and my aspirations to study professionally had to be postponed.

At **18 years old**, I embarked on my first **business venture**. To contribute financially, I took up **direct selling** of beauty and health products, an industry largely dominated by **female entrepreneurs** at the time. I invested in a **full Reeva Beauty make-up kit**, fully financed, as my first major business expense. It was daunting to take on that financial commitment at such a young age, but it was a means to an end at the time.

This experience was my **first real taste of business ownership**—it taught me about **financial responsibility, self-discipline, and the power of direct sales** to create independence. Just a year later, at **19**, an extraordinary **business opportunity** came my way. The **women's boutique** where I had been working at the time was up for sale. I had gained valuable experience managing **marketing**

**and sales** and had established strong relationships with clients and boutique owners across nearby towns through a **consignment-based model**. Recognising my potential, the boutique owner, facing personal upheaval, offered me a **once-in-a-lifetime opportunity** to **buy the business through a monthly repayment plan**. I had no capital or collateral, but I had a work ethic, a vision, and an opportunity I couldn't ignore.

Taking ownership of the boutique was both **exciting and overwhelming**. Balancing **client payments, supplier costs, and cash flow** became my **biggest challenge**. With no formal background in **fashion design**, I took a bold step and **established a factory shop**, employing **ten seamstresses** to create **bespoke designs**. The demand was high, but so was the **financial pressure**. Every order required reinvestment, and strikes and labour tensions disrupted production and delayed payments. There were times when I questioned whether I had taken on too much.

## 1.3 Lessons learned: Personal growth, leadership, and purpose

As my boutique and factory shop grew, I recognised the need for **expansion and financial backing**. I entered a **partnership with a woman 15 years my senior**, who promised to provide funding to scale the business. However, **her intentions were not pure**. The partnership was short-lived, and she **disappeared with most of the**

**stock**, leaving me with **substantial debt**—all of which was in my name.

This **betrayal was a harsh lesson** in business, trust, and financial risk. I had no choice but to **refinance the debt and push forward**. Despite the financial strain, I **refused to give up** and continued running both the boutique and factory shop. This boutique and factory shop experience became my first real test as an entrepreneur, reinforcing the importance of financial planning, risk management, and adaptability—lessons that would **shape my future in the financial industry**.

My **strong relationship with my bank manager** opened the door to a new opportunity. I was offered a position as a trainee financial adviser, making me the **youngest adviser-in-training** at the bank, nationally. At the time, the industry was still self-regulated, governed by the **Life Offices Association**, an agreement among insurance companies.

Although it came without a fixed salary, I could generate my own income based on the number of appointments and effort put in, providing me with financial stability and the chance to develop new skills. I immersed myself in **every available training programme**, eventually earning recognition as the youngest financial planner in the bank for a few years and achieving national success in cross-selling initiatives. This period was tough. The industry was male-dominated, and **women were not recognised as**

**taxpayers** or owners of financial products. When legislation **changed in 1995, I seized the moment. Hosting information sessions for women, I educated them** on opening their own bank accounts, contributing to their own retirement annuities, insuring against life's adversities, drawing up wills, and understanding their marriage regime and the risks it poses.

Over time, the financial services landscape shifted. Following the merger of four major banks, adviser roles were consolidated, and responsibilities reallocated. Despite my experience and previous success, I had to re-establish myself, often facing scepticism because of my age.

I decided to join a Johannesburg stock exchange (JSE)-listed financial services company, which previously supported my efforts and campaigns to educate women in my capacity as a financial adviser. They appointed me and two of my team members from the bank, **which I was responsible for at the time**

When financial planning became a legislated profession in 2001, I completed the **Certified Financial Planner** qualification, marking a turning point in my career. This shift reinforced my belief that financial independence is the foundation of security and opportunity, particularly for women.

**In 1992, I married my wonderfully supportive husband,**

who has always encouraged my **ambitions and success**. His unwavering belief in my potential gave me the **confidence to explore new opportunities**, knowing that I had a strong and **equal partner by my side**. When his career required relocation to Durban in 2001, we made the move with our two children, at a time when my career was flourishing.

**Starting over** in a new market was no easy task. Despite still working for the same company in a similar position, the pace was much slower, and I had to rebuild my client base from scratch. Though it was tough to do the same level of business and compete with Johannesburg and other teams on a national scale, it was also a lifesaver and forced us to lead a more balanced life, and we grew much closer as a family. Our children **adapted to their new environment,** attending extra English lessons, and we focused on integrating into our new community through church and school sports.

Despite the challenges, I **remained determined**. Competing at a **national level**, especially against the **high-performance teams in Johannesburg and Pretoria**, required me to **adjust my approach**. I focused more on administrators in offices to change the sales process and behaviour of the new panel of financial advisers. This program supported my efforts and rendered me successful again and again in different roles. I encouraged colleagues to adopt a similar process so that they qualified as well and trained all that were interested In other positions later in my career, this strategy repeatedly turned teams and sales performance around.

I have always believed that **hard work, perseverance, and continuous learning** are the keys to success. My journey in the financial services industry has been a testament to that belief.

In **2004**, I stepped into a **regional leadership position**. At the time, the **franchise was underperforming**, but through **strategic leadership, mentorship, and recruiting dynamic new talent**, we **turned it around and outperformed our competitors year after year**. Many of the business consultants I led went on to achieve national recognition and prestigious international **incentive trips**— a milestone that reaffirmed our collective success.

In 2010, I accepted the position of **key individual and regional manager, overseeing two provinces** at another **JSE-listed financial advisory company** after a national acquisition of stockbrokers. In **2014**, I transferred to the **Western Cape** to take on new professional responsibilities after two male colleagues resigned at the same time. It also provided me and my husband the opportunity to be closer to our children, who were both studying at **Stellenbosch University** at the time.

One of my most **personally fulfilling milestones** came in **2018**, when I completed my long-aspired **MBA** at the **University of Stellenbosch Business School**. It was a moment of **immense pride**, made even more special because I graduated on the **same day, from the same faculty, as both my son and daughter**—each pursuing their own professional careers.

*Family graduation day! A proud day indeed, when my children and I all graduated from Stellenbosch University on the same day, same faculty.*

Looking back, I can **deeply relate** to Giorgio Armani's words: 'My virtues and attributes are the same. I am a bad loser, and therefore, I try to not find myself in that position.'

### A message to women: The purpose of this book

This book does not provide **financial advice**—it is a **blueprint for empowerment.** I want to help **women navigate their financial journey,** understand their **rights and opportunities,** and **take control of their future.** Financial independence is **not about rebelling** against traditions or relationships—it is about **creating equal opportunities** and ensuring that **women have the knowledge and confidence to shape their own financial destinies.**

**Many women before us have fought for the rights we now have.** It is time to **embrace and build upon the progress they made.** By understanding **financial planning, investment strategies, and legal protections,** women can

- secure their financial future,
- support their families with confidence,
- leave a legacy for future generations, and
- contribute meaningfully to society.

Through the years, I have come to understand that **success is not just about achievement; it is also about self-awareness, self-forgiveness, healing, and faith.**

My **father's suicide** left me with **deep-rooted feelings of guilt and questions, a relentless drive for achievement, and a pursuit of external validation**—the belief that one must always perform at the highest level to be accepted and that there are **no second chances in life.** This mindset, while pushing me toward excellence, also made me **rush through life without pausing to celebrate my successes.** Over time, and after making my own mistakes in life, I realised that this **need for constant achievement** was not the key to true fulfilment. Instead, I found **solace and wisdom in my faith.**

I learned that **God's grace is ever-present,** and **failures are not final**—they are **stepping stones toward understanding ourselves and His greater purpose for us.** Though we cannot always **see His plan for the future,** we can **look back and recognise His hand in our past,** as He closed a door when we were relentlessly *'killing'* ourselves in trying to achieve a pre-set goal or fix a situation, and could not see the many better opportunities or a different path that He provided.

Six years ago, I took another leap forward by investing in a consultancy franchise. We distribute market-leading financial products on behalf of a JSE-listed insurance company, working with financial advisers to equip them with tools to help their clients. This venture has deepened my understanding of financial strategies, building trusted relationships and has reaffirmed my commitment to empowering others—especially women.

My **children's professional achievements** also inspire me. My **daughter and her husband, who are both professionally qualified, currently live apart in different provinces due to work responsibilities.** She is a permanently employed mother with two young children, and he manages family responsibilities during the week in Johannesburg and travels home to Cape Town on weekends. Like so many women today, my daughter is **balancing career aspirations with her role as a mother,** striving to **reach the pinnacle of her profession,** while **maintaining family stability.**

Both my **son and his wife are very successful chartered accountants abroad.** Their journeys remind me that **financial independence is not just about money**—it is about **living a balanced life, taking charge of your finances, building the life you envision, making informed decisions, and securing a future for the next generation.**

1.4 Key takeaways

## 1. Early Life Lessons Shaped by Faith and Resilience

Strong Christian values, high parental expectations, and early experiences of adversity helped build a foundation of perseverance, work ethic, and spiritual grounding.

## 2. Financial Vulnerability Starts at Home

The sudden loss of a breadwinner exposed a lack of financial preparedness—outdated estate planning, policy gaps, and dependence on a single income had devastating effects on the family's financial security.

## 3. Gender Roles and Systemic Disempowerment

Entrenched societal norms and legal structures placed financial control in male hands, leaving women financially dependent, unprepared, and unprotected during crises.

## 4. The High Cost of Limited Financial Literacy

Without basic knowledge of finance, investments, or insurance, navigating hardship became even harder—highlighting the urgent need for financial education, especially for women.

## 5. Family Adversity Sparked a Drive for Financial Empowerment

Loss and hardship planted the seed for future independence, inspiring a lifelong commitment to financial resilience and planning.

## 6. Entrepreneurship as a Path to Independence

Early exposure to business through direct selling and running a boutique taught hands-on lessons in resourcefulness, problem-solving, and personal agency.

## 7. Lessons Learned from Failure and Transition

Business betrayal and financial setbacks underscored the importance of legal knowledge, due diligence, and adaptability—paving the way for a new career in financial services.

## 8. Education and Professional Growth as Tools of Empowerment

Pursuing qualifications like the CFP® and MBA was transformational, helping to break gender barriers in finance and demonstrating the power of continuous learning.

## 9. Personal Growth, Supportive Relationships, and Faith

A strong marriage, respect for one another, a commitment to parenting, and deep faith provided emotional and spiritual support through life's highs and lows, reinforcing resilience and purpose.

## 10. A Mission to Educate and Empower Women Financially

This journey fuels a passion to simplify finance for women, challenge traditional stereotypes, and build a legacy of financial independence, education, and empowerment for future generations.

# Chapter 2: The Changing Role of Women in Society and Finance

In recent decades, the role of women in society has undergone a profound transformation. From access to education and legal rights to entrepreneurship and digital finance, women have more tools than ever before to shape their financial futures. And yet, progress in opportunity does not always translate into progress in confidence or control.

This section explores the key societal shifts that have created the current landscape—and highlights the urgent call for women to act, engage, and lead financially.

## 2.1 Educational attainment and workforce participation

Women are now more educated than ever before. According to the United Nations Educational, Scientific, and Cultural Organization (UNESCO), the global literacy rate for young women (ages 15–24) has increased from 79% in 1995 to 91.5% in 2023. In many countries, women now enrol in and graduate from universities at higher rates than men, equipping themselves with the skills and knowledge needed to pursue diverse and higher-paying careers.

Since the 1950s, the percentage of women in the workforce has nearly doubled. Today, women make up almost half of the global labour force, including a significant portion in South Africa. This participation has fuelled global economies and driven change at every level of society.

**Why it matters**

- Income creates autonomy.
- Women reinvest in their families and communities.
- More women working = more collective financial power.

**But participation alone doesn't equal ownership. Too many women still**

- lack access to leadership roles.
- earn less than men for the same work.
- remain financially dependent despite earning income.

Encouraging workforce participation is no longer enough— we must also ensure that women are **building wealth, making decisions**, and **claiming their space** in long-term financial planning.

## 2.2 Challenging stereotypes, bias, and financial exclusion

Despite progress, **historical biases and discriminatory norms** still shape **perceptions of gender roles**, particularly in male-dominated industries. These biases—ingrained through **social norms, policies, and power structures**—continue to affect women's career choices and financial opportunities, and, while education creates opportunity, it doesn't guarantee **financial security**. Even highly educated women often defer financial decisions to others due to a lack of confidence, cultural conditioning, or limited practical financial literacy. In regions like sub-Saharan Africa, socio-economic barriers such as early marriage, limited access to quality education, and financial constraints still limit many young women's potential.

## 2.3 Local and global legal progress

Legal systems around the world have made strides toward gender equality. Treaties like **CEDAW** (1979) laid the global groundwork, while national reforms—like **South Africa's recognition of women as taxpayers in 1995**—further advanced financial autonomy.

**Other key milestones include:**

- The Employment Equity Act (No. 55 of 1998): Combating discrimination in the workplace.
- Labour Relations (No. 66 of 1995) and Basic Conditions of Employment (No. 75 of 1997) Acts: Protecting maternity rights and workplace equality.
- Property and inheritance laws: Now allowing women to own, inherit, and manage assets independently.

These changes are critical—but they're only useful when women know about them and enforce them. Financial dependence, cultural pressures, and lack of access to advice still prevent many from fully exercising their rights. Legal advancements provide the foundation for financial independence, but women must take active steps to educate themselves, enforce their rights, and take control of their finances.

## 2.4 Entrepreneurship and financial inclusion

The rise of mobile banking and digital finance has transformed access to money—especially for women in rural or underserved communities. No longer reliant on brick-and-mortar banks, many now have access to savings tools, investment platforms, and small business credit.

**With these tools, women can**

- leave abusive relationships without economic fear.
- invest in their children's education.
- start businesses and build generational wealth.

But digital access isn't enough **without education**. Many women still lack confidence, and too few institutions offer gender-sensitive financial guidance.

**The solution:** Tailored literacy, practical tools, and intentional outreach.

Women around the world are launching businesses, disrupting industries, and leading innovation. The **Global Entrepreneurship Monitor** reports a steady increase in female-led ventures—with profound ripple effects on families and communities. In fact, women entrepreneurs often reinvest up to 90% of their income back into their households.

However, **systemic challenges remain**:

- Access to capital and fair lending is limited.
- Many women operate in lower-profit sectors.
- Networks and mentorship opportunities are scarce.

The number of women in national parliaments has more than doubled since 1995. In South Africa, women now hold 46% of National Assembly seats—a significant step toward inclusive decision making. But representation hasn't always translated into economic empowerment. Many women in leadership roles still

- lack financial education.
- do not shape policy to address women's unique financial needs.
- struggle with access to investment resources themselves.

We need financially informed leaders—women who understand not only governance, but how economic systems must evolve to serve future generations of women.

*Representation is a start. Participation in financial policymaking is the goal.*

## 2.5 Seizing the moment: Women must claim their power

Today's woman has unprecedented access to education, careers, and financial rights, yet progress is not automatic—it demands action. Knowledge is power, and women must educate themselves on their financial rights and options, financial management, investments, and wealth-building strategies, using that expertise not only to secure their own future but to influence economic policy that benefits future generations. Legal advancements have opened doors in politics, finance, and business, but these opportunities must be actively pursued, implemented, and enforced to create lasting change. This means

- taking control of your earnings,
- building wealth for the long term,
- using the legal and tax tools, products, services, and platforms available,
- challenging limiting beliefs and gendered expectations,
- advocating for systems that support your goals, and
- fostering peer networks that amplify collective success.

*Access means little without action; now is the time to turn opportunity into power.*

The financial system must **evolve** to support women entrepreneurs with

- gender-equitable funding models,
- strategic mentorship opportunities, and
- products tailored to female-led businesses.

The financial sector must also recognise and address the **specific needs of female clients**. Advisers and institutions **must focus on understanding the female perspective and establish a trust relationship. They must play an active role** in ensuring **women receive tailored financial guidance and investment opportunities**, and take female clients' specific **marriage regime** and associated risks and responsibilities into consideration when providing financial services to women.

## 2.6 Key takeaways

***Education and workforce participation are improving, but not enough:*** Women have made remarkable strides in education and are joining the workforce in record numbers. However, participation doesn't guarantee empowerment. Many still lack leadership roles, equal pay, and true financial independence. Income is just the beginning; long-term wealth building and financial decision making are critical.

*Stereotypes and bias still limit women's financial confidence:* Deep-rooted cultural norms and gender biases continue to shape women's roles and financial behaviour. Even highly educated women may lack confidence or defer financial decisions to others. Financial literacy and empowerment must address emotional, cultural, and psychological barriers—not just provide information.

*Legal progress is meaningful—but underutilised:* Global and local legal reforms have given women more rights in the workplace, property ownership, and financial matters. These rights are only powerful when women are aware of them and willing (and able) to enforce them. Legal frameworks are the foundation; real change requires awareness, education, and execution.

*Digital finance and entrepreneurship are powerful equalisers:* Mobile banking and digital tools have opened up access to financial services, especially in underserved communities. Female entrepreneurs are driving social change and reinvesting in families and communities. Yet, challenges persist: limited access to capital, lack of mentorship, and industries that remain male-dominated.

*Representation without economic empowerment is not enough:* Political representation has grown, but financial education and influence among women leaders still lag. True empowerment means shaping financial policies and systems that reflect and support women's realities. Women leaders must be financially informed to drive lasting, systemic change.

*Now is the time for women to seize financial power:* Access must translate into action: managing money, investing, building wealth, and influencing economic systems. The financial system must evolve to offer gender-responsive products, advice, and support structures. Financial institutions and advisers have a responsibility to understand women's specific needs and offer tailored guidance.

# Chapter 3: Understanding the Psychology of Money

Mind Over Money: The Emotional Barriers to Financial Confidence

Financial independence isn't just about understanding spreadsheets, policies, or investment products—it begins with what's happening inside our minds and hearts. Before we explore practical strategies for financial planning, we must acknowledge the invisible forces that often hold us back—our thoughts, emotions, and past experiences. Much of this book has touched on the confidence gap, cultural messages, and generational patterns that shape women's financial behaviour. But it's worth pausing to summarise the core emotional roadblocks many women still face:

- Fear of making a mistake
- Shame over financial struggles
- Cultural expectations to defer to men
- Emotional spending or avoidance

Financial freedom requires more than tools—it requires courage. This section explores the deeply rooted beliefs, fears, and societal conditioning that quietly influence women's financial behaviours—and how shifting our mindset is just as important as building our savings.

## 3.1 Emotional legacies of money and cultural conditioning

From a young age, many of us are subtly taught that money is something men grow, and women manage. As little girls, we are encouraged to save and be careful, while boys are praised for taking risks and investing boldly.

This emotional inheritance runs deep—especially in families where money was a source of tension, secrecy, or control. Guilt, fear, or shame about money can linger for decades. For some women, financial success even feels uncomfortable or disloyal, especially if they surpass their parents' or partner's achievements.

In many homes, financial discussions were handled by the father, or not discussed at all. As a result, countless women enter adulthood with limited exposure to budgeting, investing, or planning. Some learned that asking financial questions was 'disrespectful' or 'unfeminine'. Others were told outright that money wasn't their responsibility.

It's time to challenge those beliefs. Being informed about your finances is not controlling—it's courageous. It's not about undermining your partner—it's about protecting your future and your family.

## 3.2 The confidence gap and financial avoidance

Research consistently shows that women are just as competent as men when it comes to financial decision making. The issue is not ability—it's confidence. Women often underestimate their own financial acumen, delaying investment decisions or deferring to others even when they themselves are more than capable. We must stop waiting until we 'know everything' before we take the first step. Competence grows with action. Start small, but do start!

Many women use money to soothe emotions—spending when stressed, giving away more than they can afford, or avoiding bank statements out of anxiety. Others hold on too tightly, afraid to invest or enjoy the fruits of their labour. Learning to recognise emotional triggers around money—and responding with grace instead of guilt—is a key part of financial empowerment.

## 3.3 Rewriting your money story

To move forward, we must rewrite the stories we've told ourselves:

- From *'I'm bad with money'* to *'I'm learning to build wealth'*.
- From *'He handles the finances'* to *'We are partners in this'*.
- From *'I don't know where to start'* to *'Today is a great day to begin'*.

Embrace growth. This isn't about having all the answers—it's about having the courage to ask the right questions.

## 3.4 Key takeaways

- **Financial confidence begins in the mind**, not the bank account.
- **Cultural conditioning**, fear of judgement, and low confidence often prevent women from stepping into financial leadership.
- **Emotional habits around money**—whether avoidance, guilt, or overspending, it can be unlearned and replaced with healthier behaviours. Start where you are, with what you have.

# PART II: BARRIERS AND BREAKTHROUGHS

## Chapter 4: Breaking the Cycle of Exclusion

For generations, **women have been constrained by cultural norms, legal restrictions, and societal expectations** that have limited their access to financial decision making. Although legislative changes have opened new doors, many of these barriers still exist—often in more subtle, internalised ways.

### 4.1 The legacy of financial exclusion

**Historically, women** were **not recognised as independent financial entities.** Men predominated financial decisions, with women seen as **secondary earners** or dependents. In South Africa, prior to **1995, only men could claim tax deductions for dependents**—legally reinforcing the idea that women were not financial contributors in their own right. **Property and inheritance laws** also often excluded women from directly owning assets, hindering wealth accumulation and generational legacy planning. **The impact is that** many women **still lack confidence** in managing finances. **Social conditioning**

discourages women from actively engaging in financial matters, and **reliance on male partners** for financial decision making continues, even among professionally qualified women.

While **legal reforms** have improved women's rights, the **real challenge** lies in **changing mindsets**—both within society and among women themselves.

## 4.2 Education: The first step towards empowerment

**Financial literacy** is the foundation of financial freedom. However, women have often been excluded from early and practical education.

**Challenges include:**

- The belief that **financial planning isn't relevant** to them, especially if they rely on a spouse or partner.
- Many were **not taught financial literacy at home or school** and have the perception that it is too complex.
- A lack of exposure to budgeting, investing, or credit management from a young age.

**The solution:**

- Make financial education accessible and relatable.
- Financial education should be practical, demonstrating

real-life applications through storytelling and case studies.

- Women should be encouraged to ask questions, seek advice from professionals, and take an active role in financial decision making.

---

*Finance isn't just for experts—it's for every woman who wants to secure her future and build the life she envisions.*

---

## 4.3 Confidence: The missing ingredient

Many women underestimate their financial abilities and lack confidence.

**Why does this happen?**

- Societal conditioning teaches women to focus on family and caregiving rather than finances and career planning.
- Fear of failure leads to avoidance of investment and financial planning.
- Stereotypes about women being 'bad with money' persist, despite research showing women often make more conservative, long-term financial decisions than men.

**Breaking the cycle:**

Seeking professional financial advice is not a sign of weakness but rather a step towards empowerment. Taking small, intentional steps, such as setting a budget, opening a savings account, or investing, builds confidence over time.

## 4.4 The way forward: A new financial mindset

Empowerment is a process, not a one-time event. **Women must:**

- educate themselves intentionally.
- challenge **outdated narratives** about their financial competence.
- take control of financial planning rather than relying on someone else.
- use available resources (books, workshops, mentorship and financial advisers) to make informed decisions.
- lead by example to empower the next generation of women (daughters, mothers, and peers), normalising financial literacy and ownership.

---

*The future of women's financial independence depends not just on laws and policies but on each woman's decision to take control of her own financial destiny.*

---

4.5 Key takeaways

## 1. The Legacy of Exclusion Still Shapes Today's Financial Behaviors

Although legal reforms have expanded women's rights, historical exclusion from property ownership, inheritance, and tax benefits continue to affect women's financial confidence and decision-making. Many women still internalize outdated beliefs that finance is a male domain.

## 2. Financial Literacy is the First Step to Empowerment

Many women were never taught financial skills and often view money management as complex or irrelevant to their lives. Making financial education accessible, relatable, and practical is key to helping women engage confidently with money matters.

## 3. Confidence – Not Competence – is the Missing Link

Women often underestimate their financial capabilities due to societal conditioning and fear of failure. Despite being prudent long-term planners, many avoid financial planning due to a lack of self-belief. Building confidence through small, consistent actions is vital.

## 4. Financial Empowerment Requires a Mindset Shift

True change comes from within. Women need to intentionally challenge limiting beliefs, take control of their financial futures, and actively participate in planning—rather than relying on partners or family members.

## 5. Educated Women Empower Generations

When women lead by example in financial decision-making, they normalize financial literacy and confidence for future generations. Empowered women can uplift their daughters, sisters, and communities by demonstrating that finance is for everyone.

# Chapter 5: Navigating Legal and Financial Systems

During my MBA studies, I conducted research on **women's attitudes towards financial planning**. The findings from that study continue to shape the insights I share in this book. While **many women successfully run businesses**, too many still overlook the legal and financial frameworks that protect their wealth. Understanding **financial structures, tax laws, marital regimes, and legal frameworks** is essential to ensure their assets are properly protected.

In this chapter, I draw on that research to provide a **grounded, practical perspective** on how **legislation has influenced women's financial decision making** and what steps they can take to **secure their financial future**.

## 5.1 Historical context: Taxation and legal barriers

Financial independence is not just an aspiration—it is a necessity. **Women who take control of their finances** are better equipped to handle life's uncertainties, make informed decisions, and secure their futures. However, achieving financial independence requires **overcoming historical, legal, and societal barriers**, including **a lack of financial literacy, ingrained gender norms, and limited access to financial resources.**

For decades, **outdated tax systems and legal barriers** have placed women at a disadvantage – undermining their autonomy and reinforcing dependency on men. These policies, deeply rooted in **historical gender norms**, were not merely inconvenient; they shaped the way women viewed themselves as earners and savers and the way in which they made investments.

Before the **1990s**, married couples in South Africa were taxed as a **single unit**. A wife had no legal identity of her own–her earnings, tax and obligations, and financial rights were effectively absorbed by her spouse, which **reinforced financial dependence**. Even as more women entered the workforce, the tax system **failed to acknowledge their economic contributions**.

This outdated model had **deep and lasting effects**:

- **Marriage in community of property**: Once married, a woman's property was legally absorbed into her husband's estate, positioning him as the financial gatekeeper and preventing her from managing assets independently.
- **Contractual limitations:** Women could not enter into contracts (e.g. buying property, taking out loans, starting businesses) or sell assets without their husband's consent.

# The Shift from Traditional Pension Plans to Individual Financial Responsibility

Historically, baby boomers relied heavily on **employer-sponsored defined benefit (DB) pension plans**. These plans provided guaranteed **predictable income** and **protected individuals from financial risk** by using a fixed factor over the *years of service*, to determine an outcome (amount) for retirement.

**Since 1995,** there has been a **global shift towards individual retirement annuities and defined contribution (DC) plans,** placing the responsibility for retirement saving squarely on the individual. Unlike DB plans, these require individuals to be actively involved in managing their investments throughout their working years as there are no fixed amount or guaranteed amount to be paid at retirement and they need to engage in regular saving, make sound investment choices, and plan effectively for retirement drawdowns (decumulation).

The decline of public welfare funding and rising healthcare costs make financial planning more complex and essential, particularly for women who face greater pressure to independently secure their financial futures. The 2008 financial crisis further revealed the risks of poor financial literacy that can lead to long-term hardship.

- **Divorce vulnerability:** Because their income and assets were legally tied to their spouse, women were often left financially disadvantaged after divorce.
- **Business exclusion:** Female entrepreneurs were often excluded from credit or legal protections due to contractual restrictions.
- **Cultural and social norms**: Gender stereotypes have reinforced male dominance in financial decision making, with many women still deferring financial control to their partners.
- **Financial literacy gap**: The lack of financial education remains a key barrier to achieving true financial independence.

Reforms in **financial and contract law** have given women

- The right to independently own property.
- The ability to enter into contracts without male approval.
- Stronger financial autonomy in marriage and divorce.

**These reforms meant that** women have **gained full control over their earnings and assets** and can invest without relying on male approval. They can **build credit histories** in their own names and enter partnerships. They are also no longer **penalised for earning their own income.**

## 5.2 Other challenges

Despite legal advances, financial inequality persists due to deeply rooted gender stereotypes, societal expectations, and structural barriers.

### *A personal perspective*

I personally experienced this when I took over the role of regional manager in Cape Town after two male colleagues resigned at the same time to open their own business. **I was transferred to fill both of their roles and oversee the entire Western Cape area, without any additional compensation.**

I faced the same challenge again when I negotiated the terms of my franchise. Despite being more qualified than my predecessor, with a very successful track-record, I was initially offered **40% less in monthly remuneration.** After negotiating, I secured equal pay— only to discover the ongoing **fee structure had been adjusted** to reflect an 'urban' base, which reduced fee income by about **30%**. The organisation has recognised my efforts, performance, and commitment and recently offered an opportunity to potentially increase income over the long-term, based on performance.

**Lesson:** Know your worth. Research salary benchmarks. Negotiate assertively and push for pay transparency.

This section explores the systemic discrimination that shaped women's financial roles and highlights the importance of knowledge and proactive legal reform to change that.

### 5.2.1 Cultural norms and early conditioning

- Lusardi & Mitchell (2014) reported that women are less likely to engage in financial planning because of traditional expectations that men should provide financially.
- Financial discussions in families tend to focus more on sons than daughters, reinforcing the belief that financial management is a male responsibility.
- A general belief and expectation exists that a woman will remarry after the death of her spouse or in the event of a divorce, and thus, inheritance will be lost to the original family.

### 5.2.2 Lower savings and financial access

Demirguc-Kunt, Klapper & Singer (2013) found that women are **less likely to have a bank account, borrow money, or invest** because of lower income levels, fewer formal employment opportunities, and limited access to financial education.

### 5.2.3 Balancing work and home responsibilities

McKeen & Bujaki (1994) noted that professional women face unique financial pressures, often expected to balance careers, caregiving, and household duties. The lack of childcare facilities and societal expectations further complicate women's financial independence.

## 5.2.4 Workplace inequality and the glass ceiling

Women still face unequal pay and limited career advancement. Segar & White (1992) argued that financial literacy programmes alone will not eliminate gender-based financial inequality without shifting power relations.

## 5.2.5 The gender pay gap

The gender pay gap remains a major obstacle to women's financial independence. Despite progress, women continue to earn less than men—a disparity that impacts their ability to accumulate wealth, invest, and secure financial stability in retirement.

**The American Association of University Women (2023) reported that** women working full-time year-round earned only 83% of what men earned (a drop from 84% in 2022), and that one year after college, women earn around 80% of men's salaries, but this gap widens to 69% after ten years. At the current pace of change, gender pay equality may only be achieved by 2159! In **South Africa**, women continue to earn **significantly less** than men. This wage inequality reinforces **financial dependency** and limits economic growth for both individuals and the nation.

**The unexplained gender pay gap:** Even after accounting for education, experience, and occupation, a portion of the wage gap cannot be explained—suggesting bias and systemic discrimination in salary structures.

**Why it matters**

- Lower salaries mean fewer opportunities for investment, asset acquisition, and retirement savings.
- Women are less likely to accumulate property and long-term assets.
- Retirement benefits, life insurance, and disability coverage are often based on earnings, putting women at a disadvantage in old age.

## 5.2.6 Life expectancy

Women typically live longer than men, meaning they need more financial resources to sustain their retirement years. However, older women are less prepared for retirement than men. Because of the disproportionately low financial literacy among women, they are vulnerable to inadequate retirement savings, high-interest debt, and risky mortgage defaults due to poor credit management.

Life expectancy in South Africa is **60.3 years for men** and **67.3 years for women** (Statistics South Africa, 2023). While this reflects a significant improvement due to advances in healthcare, early detection, and healthier living, these averages should not form the sole basis for retirement planning. It is wiser to plan for a longer life span to ensure long-term financial security.

**Why this matters**

- Women are more likely to outlive their partners, meaning they may have to fund **more years in retirement** alone.
- **Medical advances** may skew the averages substantially as people tend to live longer, i.e. into their 80s and 90s, and this will increase even more over time.
- The **cost of healthcare and long-term care** increases with age, requiring careful planning.
- Women must proactively manage their financial resources to ensure long-term security.
- Societal expectations may limit women's **access to inherited wealth**—especially under outdated cultural assumptions that women will remarry and thus don't 'need' family assets.

**Financial strategies for longevity**

- **Start investing early** to benefit from compound interest.
- **Prioritise retirement savings** through annuities, pension plans, and long-term investments. The later you start, the more you need to invest.

- **Consider healthcare and long-term care insurance;** medical costs increase significantly in later years.
- **Understand inheritance laws and estate planning:** Know your rights regarding property and assets.

### 5.2.7 Barriers to career advancement

Despite equal qualifications, women are often passed over for promotions, earn less, and face systemic barriers that hinder career growth. These include

- **Occupational segregation:** Male-dominated industries pay more than female-dominated ones, despite similar skill requirements.
- **Gender bias in leadership:** Women are underrepresented in executive roles.
- **Limited investment in training:** Employers spend less on upskilling women.
- **Career breaks for caregiving:** Maternity leave and childcare reduce opportunities for advancement and delay promotions.

In Australia, the gender pay gap in financial services, real estate, and insurance industries is 23%, largely due to these barriers.

**How to overcome these barriers**

- **Advocate for equal pay:** Transparency in salaries can close gender wage gaps.
- **Seek professional development:** Ongoing training and certifications can help bridge the leadership gap.
- **Challenge bias in promotions:** Companies must recognise and address unconscious bias in hiring and advancement.

## 5.2.8 The motherhood penalty

Women often experience financial setbacks due to bias against mothers in the workplace. Employers prefer child-free women over mothers when hiring, and women earn less after having children, while men receive a *'fatherhood bonus'*, often being promoted or given raises for the additional responsibilities. In the US, ten years after graduating from college, 23% of mothers are out of the workforce, and 17% work part-time, compared with only 1% of fathers.

**Why this matters**

The wage gap worsens for mothers, affecting lifetime earnings and retirement savings. The financial burden of childcare often falls disproportionately on women.

Time away from work reduces lifetime earnings and retirement savings.

**Solutions**

- **Negotiate for a competitive salary:** Don't accept lower pay based on personal circumstances.
- **Invest early in retirement and assets:** Plan ahead for income gaps due to maternity leave.
- **Push for family-friendly policies in the workplace:** Flexible work, parental leave, and childcare subsidies.
- If you do have a partner, **ensure equal responsibilities**.

## 5.2.9 Marital status and financial vulnerability

As family structures evolve, women are increasingly becoming the primary or sole breadwinners, but they remain more financially vulnerable due to structural inequalities.

In **the US** (2020), 40% of households with children under 18 had mothers as primary earners, and 69% of mothers were primary, sole, or co-breadwinners. In **South Africa** (2018), 42% of households were headed by women, and 30% of employed women were the primary earners in their families.

**Key financial risks for women**

- **Higher debt burden:** Women are more likely to co-sign loans or take on debt for their families.

- **Lower savings and investments:** Due to lower earnings and financial responsibilities, women save less.
- **Slow financial recovery post-divorce or separation:** Women recover financially more slowly than men after separation.

**Solutions:**

- **Build an emergency fund** to maintain stability in uncertain times (3–6 months of expenses).
- **Invest in long-term assets:** Ensure ownership of property and retirement funds.
- **Be proactive in financial planning:** Understanding tax laws, credit scores, and estate planning can secure financial independence.

## 5.2.10 The financial impact of divorce

Divorce is one of the biggest financial disruptors for women. With divorce rates on the rise, women need to clearly understand how their property settlement will be determined, which is based on their marital regime. Child and spousal maintenance are negotiated based on lifestyle, income, and expenses.

**The cost of divorce** (Global and SA Trends)

- **A 30% increase in income is needed** post-divorce to maintain the same standard of living.

- **83% of children live with their mother** post-divorce, increasing financial strain.
- **20% of women fall into poverty** due to divorce.
- **75% of women do not receive child support**—a major financial risk.

## In South Africa:

- There are **33 divorces per 100,000** people (2022).
- **Women initiate more divorces than men**, often due to financial strain.
- **56% of divorces involve children under 18** years old, adding economic pressure.
- **21% of divorced women are unemployed** at the time of separation.

## Key challenges

- **Unequal division of assets:** Women often walk away with less.
- **Bias in maintenance judgements:** Due to gender biases, women are seen as opportunistic, not entitled, when they claim spousal and child maintenance.
- **Poor valuation of unpaid caregiving roles and missed opportunity cost:** Caregiving responsibilities often reduce women's education/earning potential, limit career progression, and create barriers to re-employment after time out of the workforce, regardless of their qualifications or experience.

- **Inconsistent child support payments:** Many fathers fail to pay.
- **Legal protections** are improving, but cultural biases still limit enforcement.

**Solutions**

- **Know your marital regime**, which affects financial settlements in divorce. More on this topic in Chapter 9, where we explore marital regimes and their financial impact.
- **Secure legal advice early in the process**: Ensure fair division of assets and maintenance payments.
- **Build financial independence before divorce:** Avoid relying on a spouse. Whether due to **wage gaps, childcare responsibilities, or divorce**, women face higher financial risks throughout life. But with the right knowledge and tools, they can protect their futures.

## 5.3 Key takeaways

- **Barriers persist:** Cultural norms, workplace inequality, and financial literacy gaps continue to hold women back.
- Divorce remains one of the **most significant events affecting women's financial stability.** Settlement outcomes depend on marital regime, and

maintenance is determined by lifestyle, income, and expenses.

- **Years spent raising children** or managing households reduce women's long-term earning potential and retirement savings, which is undervalued.
- Despite better laws, enforcement and attitudes still lag behind.
- **Solutions & Financial Empowerment**
  - **Understand your marital regime** — it defines your legal rights during divorce.
  - **Seek legal and financial advice early** to ensure fair settlements.
  - **Prioritise financial independence** before marriage and throughout life — don't rely solely on a partner.

---

*Divorce doesn't have to be a financial downfall*
*— it can be a turning point.*
*Women who understand their rights, plan early, and build independent wealth, create lasting financial security regardless of marital status.*

---

# Chapter 6: Legislative Reforms and Women's Path to Financial Autonomy

Understanding South Africa's **legal and financial frameworks** is essential for women to **secure financial independence**, especially in matters related to **marriage, divorce, retirement, and estate planning**. Women's access to financial independence has been closely tied to their **political and legal rights**. This section explores the **historical legal milestones and reforms** that shaped women's financial roles and security over time, and highlights how women can take advantage of them.

By **1932, developed nations** like the **UK** began seeing **shifts in women's roles**, influenced by

- **increased access to birth control,** allowing women greater control over their futures.
- **education reforms,** expanding opportunities for women in formal employment.
- **socialisation of domestic services:** reducing traditional caregiving burdens and freeing time for economic participation.

These changes **set the stage for legal and financial reforms**, moving towards **greater gender equality** in financial matters.

In South Africa, the 1956 Women's March—where over

20,000 women protested against pass laws—was a defining moment in the struggle for gender equality. While the march didn't immediately result in financial or legal reform, it laid the foundation for future activism and awareness. Major legal progress came with the **Matrimonial Property Act (Act 88 of 1984)**, which recognised marriage as a financial partnership and abolished the husband's marital power, granting married women greater financial autonomy. However, the **Income Tax Act (Act 58 of 1962)** continued to treat married women as financial dependents, lagging behind the broader push for gender equality and requiring urgent reform to ensure fairness in tax treatment.

These legislative shifts were further accelerated in the post-apartheid era, particularly with the **1996 Constitution**, which enshrines gender equality and non-discrimination as fundamental rights—providing the foundation for ongoing legal, economic, and social reform for South African women.

Voting rights were among the first significant steps toward gender equality. Although the US's **Comprehensive Anti-Apartheid Act of 1986** imposed economic sanctions and restrictions on the South African government in an effort to pressure it to end apartheid, the **first non-racial democratic election** in South Africa was only held in **1994**. With political inclusion came a gradual shift in gender norms and legal rights that laid the groundwork for women's financial autonomy.

*Table 6.1 The date of the granting of women's suffrage in various countries*

| Country | Year Women Gained the Right to Vote |
|---|---|
| USA | 1920 (19th Amendment) |
| UK | 1928 (Equal Franchise Act) |
| South Africa (White women) | 1930 |
| South Africa (All races) | 1994 |

## 6.1 The Push for Change: The Margo Commission and its findings

In the 1980s, the **Margo Commission** was **instrumental in pushing for tax reforms**, highlighting the inequities in joint taxation and its impact on women's financial independence. Their findings aligned with a study by the Human Sciences Research Council (1986), revealing the real-world harm.

- Women were penalised for working due to **progressive tax rates** applied to their husbands' income.
- **Men bore legal responsibility for their wives' taxes**—creating resentment and financial strain.
- Many couples **divorced** or **cohabited** to escape joint taxation.
- Skilled married women often **withdrew from the workforce,** wasting years of education and training.

These findings accelerated calls for separate taxation—

treating women as full financial individuals. The recommendations were groundbreaking.

- **Separate taxation** for men and women, giving women financial recognition in their own right.
- The elimination of gender-based tax discrimination, promoting equity, and acknowledging the evolving economic role of women.

Though slow to implement, these recommendations laid the foundation for reform that redefined women's financial status.

South Africa's tax system was modelled after the UK's, where joint taxation was also the norm. However, the UK reformed its system in 1990, introducing separate taxation to promote fairness.

## 6.2 The Income Tax Act (No. 21 of 1995)

In 1994, the Katz Commission recommended drastic changes to the Income Tax Act, leading to the elimination of gender-based tax discrimination to be implemented in **1995:**

- **Married women were taxed separately from their husbands,** recognising them as independent financial entities.

- **Women could now claim tax rebates** and **deduct contributions** to retirement annuities in their own right.
- **One universal tax rate was applied to all taxpayers**, regardless of gender or marital status.

## Why was this important?

Before these changes, women faced higher tax penalties, discouraging them from working, saving, or investing. Many withdrew from the labour force upon marriage, **resulting in lost economic potential**. In the US, women made up nearly half of the workforce, and losing educated women was economically unsustainable. South Africa faced similar challenges, and keeping women in the workforce was critical for economic growth.

## By eliminating joint taxation, women gained

- **financial autonomy**, allowing them to make independent financial decisions.
- **access to tax benefits**, enabling better retirement planning.
- **incentives to work**, increasing their participation in the economy.
- **the opportunity to build credit histories** in their own names and enter partnerships. They were no longer penalised for earning their own income.

Despite these advances, many women are still unaware of these legal changes and fail to take full advantage of them. Understanding these financial rights is crucial to building long-term wealth and security.

## 6.3 Labour law reforms

"Legislative reforms such as the **Labour Relations Act (Act No. 66 of 1995)** and the **Employment Equity Act (Act No. 55 of 1998)** laid the legal groundwork for equal workplace rights, mandating non-discrimination and promoting gender equality in hiring, promotions, and career advancement."

## 6.4 The Financial Intelligence Centre Act (No. 38 of 2001)

The enactment of the Financial Intelligence Centre Act (FICA) in 2001 was a pivotal moment in South Africa's financial regulatory framework. Primarily designed to combat money laundering, fraud, and the financing of terrorism, FICA introduced rigorous verification requirements to ensure that all financial transactions could be traced back to an identifiable individual or legal entity.

While FICA's principal aim was financial transparency and security, **it also had an unexpected—and profoundly empowering—impact on women.** Prior to this legislation, many women, particularly those in traditional or patriarchal households, operated financial accounts under their husbands' names. The widespread use of third-party payments effectively limited their financial autonomy and often excluded them from meaningful participation in household financial decisions.

With the introduction of FICA, **third-party payments became strictly regulated.** Financial institutions could no longer process transactions without first verifying the identity of the account holder. This regulatory shift made it mandatory for every individual, **including women, to open bank accounts in their own names.** What began as a compliance requirement evolved into a powerful catalyst for change.

FICA required women to step forward and claim their financial identity. **For many, it was the first time they engaged directly with banks, signed their own documentation, and gained insight into products like savings accounts, investments, and credit facilities. Women who had previously relied on others to manage their financial affairs were now taking ownership of their money and their future.**

This legislative shift extended beyond individual banking. Legal entities such as trusts and companies were also brought into the FICA framework. Trustees, directors, and beneficiaries had to be verified. **Many women, previously unaware of their roles or rights in these structures,** discovered their inclusion and began to ask questions about their financial entitlements and obligations.

FICA didn't just enforce transparency in financial systems; **it opened the door for women to develop financial literacy and autonomy.** Having a personal bank account became more than a regulatory requirement—it was a declaration of independence.

For women across South Africa, this marked a turning point. Financial independence was no longer an abstract goal—it became a practical, accessible reality. With their own accounts, women could build credit histories, apply for loans, invest, and plan for retirement. More importantly, they could do so without needing a spouse's permission or signature.

This transformation demonstrates how legislative reform, when implemented thoughtfully, can have far-reaching social impact. FICA became more than a financial security tool; it was a step toward economic justice and gender equality.

**What these reforms meant for women**

- Women **gained full control over their earnings and assets** and could invest without relying on male approval.
- They could **build credit histories** in their own names

and enter partnerships.

- They were no longer **penalised for earning their own income.**

## 6.5 The Financial Advisory and Intermediary Services Act (No. 37 of 2002) and the importance of professional financial advice

The **Financial Advisory and Intermediary Services (FAIS) Act** was established in South Africa to protect consumers by **regulating financial advisers and intermediaries.** This law ensures that financial professionals meet strict ethical and operational standards, ultimately safeguarding consumers from poor advice and unethical practices.

**Key objectives of the FAIS Act**

- **Protect policyholders:** Prevent negligent or unethical financial advice that may lead to financial loss.
- **Regulate the industry:** Ensure that all financial advisers are registered with the Financial Sector Conduct Authority (FSCA) and meet professional requirements.
- **Promote transparency:** Require full disclosure on financial products, risks, commissions, and service fees.
- **Ensure competency:** Demand ongoing education and training for advisers to stay updated on legal and financial best practices.

### Why this matters for women

- Women traditionally relied on male partners for financial decisions, making it critical for them to seek trusted financial advice.
- FAIS ensures that qualified advisers offer guidance tailored to their needs, helping them take control of their financial futures.
- Registered advisers must act in your best interest, empowering you to make informed decisions about savings, investments, and insurance.

**Tip:** Always ask your adviser:

- Are you registered with the FSCA?
- What product providers do you represent?
- Can I see a copy of your disclosure document?
- What services and financial categories are you licensed to advise on?
- How often will you review my financial plan?
- Do you take my specific marriage regime into consideration?

**What advisers provide**

Advisors provide a comprehensive **financial needs analysis**, which includes but is not limited to

- budgeting and debt planning,
- insurance needs (incl. risk cover, health insurance and gap cover),
- retirement and investment strategies (local and offshore),
- estate planning, wills, and trusts,
- tax planning

## 6.6 The Divorce and Pension Funds Acts

Updates to the Divorce (No. 70 of 1979) and the Pension Funds (No. 24 of 1956) Acts include key **provisions that protect the interests of the non-member spouse** during and after divorce.

If the couple got divorced

- **before 13 September 2007,** the member spouse (the one who owns the pension fund) would pay tax when they eventually withdraw their pension.
- **after 13 September 2007,** the non-member spouse (the one receiving a share of the pension) must pay tax on the pension portion received.

This **tax liability shift** highlights the need for **careful financial planning** during divorce negotiations.

**Section 7(8) of the Divorce Act** allows courts to **allocate a portion of the pension interest** to the **non-member spouse** upon divorce. The divorce order must **clearly specify** the division of pension benefits. **Only accrued pension interest** up to the date of divorce is included— **future retirement benefits are not covered**.

**Section 37D of the Pension Funds Act** enables pension funds to execute deductions after a court grants a valid divorce order. Once a court issues a **valid divorce order, the pension fund must comply and make the payment.**

**Risk Alert:** Vague or incorrect wording in divorce orders can delay pension payouts and result in disputes. Ensuring legal and financial guidance is crucial for securing post-divorce financial stability.

## 6.7 The Financial Services General Amendment Act (No. 22 of 2008)

This Act was introduced to align **South Africa's financial services industry** with **global financial standards** and to promote transparency and protection for consumers.

**Key benefits**

- **Stronger consumer protection** prevents misleading financial practices.
- **Financial stability and transparency** ensure proper oversight of financial institutions.
- **Pension fund benefits for divorced spouses:** A non-

**member spouse** can receive a **portion of their ex-spouse's pension fund** at the time of divorce.

### Why it matters for women

- Many women are **not the primary earners** and rely on their spouse's retirement savings.
- This law ensures that **divorced women receive a fair share** of pension benefits.
- Proper **divorce settlement planning** is crucial to securing long-term financial stability.

### 6.8   Government Employees Pension Fund (GEPF) and Divorce Settlements

- **Divorces finalized before 1 March 2012**: If the non-member spouse received a share of the pension interest through a divorce order and withdrew the funds, **no tax was payable by the non-member spouse.** The GEPF member remained liable for the tax.
- **Divorces (or payouts) on or after 1 March 2012**: Following legislative changes, **the non-member spouse receiving the payout** is now **personally liable for the tax** on their portion of the pension interest when they elect to withdraw it.

**Why this matters for women:**

Many GEPF members and non-member spouses still assume that the **old tax rules apply**, leading to **unexpected tax liabilities**. This often affects women, who may not be aware that they are responsible for the tax on their share of the pension payout. Proper legal and financial advice is essential to avoid financial strain during or after divorce settlements involving GEPF benefits.

Ensuring divorce settlements are structured with **tax in mind** is critical.

The following example will put the changes into perspective: **Case Study: Lerato's Unexpected Tax Bill**

Lerato, a 45-year-old nurse and mother of two, was married for 18 years to her husband, Thabo, a government employee and member of the **Government Employees Pension Fund (GEPF)**. During their divorce proceedings in 2021, the court awarded Lerato 40% of Thabo's pension interest in terms of the divorce order.

Assuming she would receive the full amount as stated in the order, Lerato was shocked to find that a significant portion of her payout was withheld for **tax purposes**. She had expected a lump sum of R400,000 but received only R320,000 after tax. The **R80,000 tax liability**, which she had not budgeted for, disrupted her plans to pay off debt and secure housing for her family.

**What went wrong?**

Lerato and her attorney were unaware that since **1 March 2012, non-member spouses (like Lerato)** are **liable for tax** on pension payouts from the GEPF. Prior to this, the **member (Thabo)** would have carried the tax burden.

Had Lerato received professional financial advice, she might have opted to **transfer the pension share into a retirement annuity or preservation fund**, thereby **deferring the tax** until withdrawal. This option could have preserved the full R400,000 for her future.

**Lessons Learned:**

- Divorce orders involving pensions must be handled with financial expertise.
- Non-member spouses should understand the **tax implications** before choosing a **cash payout**.
- A **direct transfer** into another retirement vehicle may be a better option to protect long-term financial security.

**Tip:** Engage both a legal and financial adviser to **calculate tax implications** and secure your future.

6.9 New legislation on maintenance payments in South Africa

Historically, maintenance payments in South Africa have been inconsistent and difficult to enforce, disproportionately affecting single mothers who rely on child support for housing, education, and healthcare.

## Challenges before the new legislation

- **Delays in legal enforcement:** Many custodial parents faced long legal battles to secure payments.
- **Lack of tracking mechanisms:** Defaulters could easily avoid making payments.
- **Weak penalties:** There were few consequences for parents who failed to pay maintenance.

## Impact on families

- **Custodial parents** (mostly women) now have **stronger legal protections** to secure reliable financial support for their children.
- **Non-paying parents face real consequences**, discouraging maintenance defaults.
- **Fewer legal hurdles** make it easier for women to enforce their children's financial rights.

*Table 6.2 Key features of the new maintenance laws*

| Feature | How it helps women |
|---|---|
| **Stronger enforcement** | Courts can now take **faster action** against non-paying parents, including **wage garnishments** and **property seizures**. |
| **Tracking defaulters** | Government agencies and **financial institutions can trace** defaulters who change addresses or jobs. |
| **Blacklisting of defaulters** | Parents who fail to pay can now **be reported to credit bureaus**, affecting their **credit scores and ability to borrow money**. |
| **Streamlined legal processes** | Courts must now **process maintenance claims more efficiently**, reducing delays. |
| **Support for low-income parents** | Courts can **assess financial situations** and set **fair** but **mandatory** payment schedules, so they can be adjusted, but remain enforceable. |

**Future considerations**

- **Implementation is key:** Success will depend on how well these laws are enforced.
- **Support services are needed:** Access to legal advice and financial resources will help custodial parents navigate these changes.

## 6.10 Illustrating societal change: Elvis Presley on *The Ed Sullivan Show*—A turning point in culture

*(my husband's contribution, an avid Elvis Presley fan)*

To better understand how societal norms evolve, let's look at an iconic moment in entertainment history: Elvis Presley's appearances on *The Ed Sullivan Show*. His journey from **controversial figure to cultural icon** mirrors the **barriers and breakthroughs** women have faced in **financial empowerment**.

Elvis made three legendary appearances on the show: 9 September and 28 October 1956 and 6 January 1957. His performances drew massive audiences and skyrocketed his fame, but they also sparked significant controversy.

### First appearance

Elvis performed live from Hollywood. He sang several songs, including 'Don't Be Cruel' and 'Love Me Tender'. This performance drew around 60 million viewers, about 82.6% of the television audience at the time. His hip-swivelling dance moves and 'suggestive' performance style were considered scandalous by many, leading to concerns about his influence on American youth. Religious and conservative groups protested, claiming his performances were obscene and morally corrupting.

## Second appearance

Elvis performed live from New York, singing hits like 'Hound Dog', 'Love Me Tender', and 'Don't Be Cruel'. Despite the controversy and backlash, his popularity continued to soar. Some religious and conservative groups called for boycotts of the show, demanding censorship of his performances. The moral debate over pop culture and youth influences intensified.

## Third appearance

By this time, the outcry had reached a peak. Elvis performed a mix of his top hits. The show's producers decided to film Elvis from the waist up to reduce controversy. This appearance is famously remembered for this censorship, which did little to diminish his appeal and instead increased it.

Despite the boycotts and censorship, Elvis' performances on *The Ed Sullivan Show* solidified his status as a cultural icon as he broke cultural barriers. His appearances are often credited with helping to bring rock 'n' roll into the mainstream. The controversy highlighted the generational divide and the growing influence of television in shaping public opinion and culture.

## The parallel journey

Elvis's story shows how conservative views can challenge cultural shifts, much like the journey towards financial empowerment for women. Just as Elvis broke barriers in music and popular culture, women are breaking barriers in financial independence and empowerment.

By understanding that traditional societal structures dictated that women couldn't own property, sign contracts, or manage their own money, women can better prepare themselves to navigate and overcome these obstacles. Education, legal awareness, resilience, and financial literacy are powerful tools in this journey.

To understand how society responds to disruptive change, consider Elvis Presley's appearances on *The Ed Sullivan Show* in the 1950s. His hip-shaking performances shocked conservative America, leading to censorship and public outrage. Yet, the attempt to limit him only amplified his influence—Elvis became a cultural icon, breaking barriers and redefining popular music.

The parallel with women's financial empowerment is striking. Just as Elvis faced backlash for challenging norms, women who claimed financial independence were often met with scepticism, criticism, or resistance. Yet, these shifts proved unstoppable. Like rock 'n' roll entering the mainstream, women's financial autonomy, once controversial, is now increasingly seen as essential.

## 6.11 Addressing ongoing changes in financial and workplace equality

Despite progress, challenges remain. Gender pay disparities, underrepresentation in leadership roles, and cultural biases continue to restrict women's financial potential.

In **2017**, **Janusz Korwin-Mikke**, a member of the European Parliament, made misogynistic statements, arguing that women should earn less than men because they are 'weaker, smaller, and less intelligent'. His outdated and offensive views were immediately condemned by other parliament members. However, his remarks reflect the **deep-rooted biases that still impact women's financial status and career growth.** Women continue to face **unfair treatment, underestimation,** and **pay gaps**—especially in male-dominated sectors. While his statements are extreme, they highlight the **continued struggle women face in workplace equality, financial independence, and professional recognition.** Gender biases still exist, even with laws in place.

**While laws have changed, real empowerment requires action.** Women must embrace financial independence and actively participate in managing their finances to break free from historical limitations. Women must embrace financial literacy, advocate for equal pay and workplace opportunities, and challenge the internalised belief that finance belongs to men. **Change is happening.** Financial literacy programmes, legal reforms, and increased workforce participation are helping women break free from financial dependency.

*Table 6.3 Summary of key lessons for women*

| Focus Area | Action Steps |
| --- | --- |
| **Financial advice** | Consult only FSCA-registered advisers<br>Request and review full disclosure documents |
| **Tax and retirement** | Start retirement planning early<br>Account for tax liabilities when structuring your portfolio |
| **Challenging bias** | Challenge stereotypes in the workplace and home<br>Educate yourself and others<br>Advocate for fair policies and equal treatment |
| **Divorce and pension settlements** | Understand your pension interest entitlement<br>Plan for tax implications<br>Ensure divorce orders are clearly and correctly worded |
| **Maintenance payments** | Use legal tools such as credit blacklisting and wage garnishment<br>Stay informed of your rights under updated laws |

When a woman controls her finances, she controls her future. Navigating legal and financial systems is not simply about compliance—it is about empowerment, resilience, and legacy.

## 6.12 Key takeaways

- **History matters:** Legal and tax systems once positioned women as financially invisible; reforms have since unlocked independence.

- **Legislation can empower:** From FICA to FAIS, legal frameworks provide tools for autonomy, transparency, and protection.

- **Advisers are allies:** Working with FSCA-registered advisers ensures safe, informed financial planning.

- **Cultural change takes time:** Like Elvis Presley challenging convention, women must persist through resistance to claim their rightful place in financial decision making.

- **Action is essential:** Laws open the door, but women must step through it by educating themselves, negotiating assertively, and actively planning for their financial futures.

- **Key actions for women to overcome financial barriers: Educate yourself** – Learn about budgeting, investing, retirement planning, and pension rights. Know your **legal rights**—and fight for them.

- **Take ownership of your finances** – Build financial independence, regardless of relationship status, and make independent financial decisions.
- **Consult a financial adviser** – Avoid financial surprises by ensuring your settlement secures your long-term future.

---

*Financial independence is not optional. It is non-negotiable.*

---

# Chapter 7: The Informal Sector – Women's Pursuit for Economic Independence

Over the past 30 years, the landscape of informal work for women has evolved significantly, offering new opportunities for financial and social independence. While traditional employment structures often limited women's participation in the workforce, the **informal sector** has provided **flexibility, autonomy, and income generation**—allowing women to **balance household responsibilities with economic empowerment**.

## 7.1 The power of the informal sector

### *7.1.1 Direct selling and party plans*

In the 1980s and 90s, direct selling became a lifeline for many women seeking to generate income while managing their home responsibilities. Companies such as Tupperware, Avon, and Reeva provided business opportunities that allowed women to sell products through social gatherings — commonly known as *party plans* that involved hosting social events at home, often after hours, where products were demonstrated and sold. Sales were driven through **word-of-mouth marketing** and **personal relationships**. The **flexible working model** allowed women to **work around family duties**.

**Tupperware: Revolutionising direct selling for women**
Tupperware parties were a global phenomenon but only came to South Africa in 1964. While Tupperware was invented by Earl Tupper in 1942, it was Brownie Wise, a pioneering woman in the company, who revolutionised its direct sales approach. She is credited with developing the Tupperware party method of selling, where women could gather socially and demonstrate products in a friendly environment, giving women an opportunity to make money while networking in their communities. The flexible nature of this business model allowed women to balance domestic duties with earning potential in the form of commission.

**Avon and Reeva**

Avon was established **in 1886 by David H. McConnell and introduced** in South Africa in 1996. Reeva Beauty & Health was established in South Africa in 1980 by Reeva Forman. These beauty companies operated similarly, empowering women to sell cosmetics and skincare products. The door-to-door sales model and hosting make-up parties allowed women to tap into their social networks while building client bases through personal relationships. It did not require significant start-up capital.

Multi-level marketing schemes became popular in the 1990s, with companies like **Herbalife, Amway, and Nu Skin** attracting many women seeking financial independence. These companies promised income based on sales commissions and recruiting new members into their teams. For example, **Herbalife** was promoted as a health and wellness company, empowering women to become distributors of nutritional supplements and emphasising personal transformation stories. Many women hosted fitness groups or wellness events to market their products. While multi-level marketing schemes gave many women a way to earn money, they also faced criticism for high upfront costs and a business model that primarily benefited those at the top of the pyramid. As a result, some women have turned to more transparent gig economy opportunities.

**The evolution of direct selling: Adapting to the digital era**

While traditional direct selling gave women an entry point into financial independence, today's digital economy has transformed how women engage in entrepreneurial opportunities. E-commerce, social media marketing, and digital networking have revolutionised informal work, allowing women to reach wider audiences with greater flexibility. Traditional home parties have evolved into online platforms and e-commerce, door-to-door sales have shifted toward social media marketing and virtual events, and printed catalogues have been replaced by digital promotions and influencer partnerships, transforming how products are showcased and sold.

## 7.1.2 Craft production, home-based work, and income generation

Many women in the past three decades have used their crafting skills to earn money from home. Activities like sewing, baking, and knitting became popular ways for women to supplement their household income.

**Sewing:** Women who were skilled with a sewing machine would take in clients for alterations or create custom garments. Some women built successful businesses around designing children's clothing, wedding attire, or uniforms for schools and businesses.

**Baking and catering:** Women often started small home-based businesses by selling baked goods or providing catering services for local events. This included everything from homemade bread to elaborate wedding cakes and catering services for small gatherings.

**Crafts:** Women also sold handmade jewellery, pottery, and knitted goods at local markets or to friends and family. Craft fairs and local markets provided opportunities for women to showcase their handmade products.

The rise of e-commerce platforms like Instagram Shop and Facebook Marketplace has expanded women's businesses from local, home-based ventures to global markets. Today, women can sell their handmade goods to an international clientele, significantly increasing their earning potential.

## 7.2 Digital entrepreneurship and the gig economy

In the past decade, technology has completely transformed how women in the informal sector earn an income. The rise of the gig economy has opened new opportunities for flexible work.

**Ridesharing and delivery apps:** With companies like **Uber** and **Bolt**, many women have found flexible, part-time work in ridesharing as independent contractors or food delivery with apps like **Uber Eats** or **UCOOK** where women can earn money on their own schedules.

**Cleaning services: Sweepsouth** connects people who need cleaning services with professional cleaners and domestic workers. Cleaners work on a per-task basis, offering flexibility for both the service provider and the client on a once-off or recurring basis.

**On-demand courier and delivery services:** Companies like **Sendr**, **Picup**, and **WumDrop** provide task-based courier services where individuals can sign up to deliver parcels. The courier gets paid per delivery, and this model has grown in line with the rise of e-commerce.

**Task-based services**: Task-based apps continue to grow in popularity in South Africa, offering flexible work and quick access to skilled help. **LUVO** is one of the latest entrants in this space. It connects users with vetted professionals for everyday services such as home cleaning, garden work, maintenance, deliveries, and even beauty services. The app is designed to be user-friendly, allowing clients to **book services, track job progress, and make payments seamlessly through the platform**. LUVO prioritises safety and professionalism by conducting background checks on service providers, and users can **rate and review** workers after each job. Available on both **Android and iOS**, it offers a practical solution for individuals looking to access or offer freelance services in a secure, convenient way. **Mystery shopping, retail audits: Field Agent** is a platform where users can complete small tasks like mystery shopping or in-store audits, and completed in exchange for payment on a per-task basis.

**E-commerce delivery partners: Takealot**, South Africa's leading e-commerce platform, partners with independent contractors for deliveries. Drivers are paid per delivery or route completed.

**Freelancing:** Websites like **M4Jam, Upwork, Freelancer** and **Fiverr** have given women access to remote freelance work in fields ranging from writing and graphic design to marketing, data capturing, product activation, and customer service. These platforms offer women the flexibility to work remotely and set their own hours by bidding on different jobs and getting paid in various currencies.

**Yaga** is a dynamic online marketplace that empowers women by offering a safe and easy way to buy and sell **new and preloved fashion**. Whether you're looking for unique, sustainable clothing or launching your own mini-boutique to sell second-hand items, Yaga helps you **earn extra income**, express your **personal style**, and support **eco-conscious living**. While its focus remains on fashion, its thriving community continues to grow as a trusted platform for women entrepreneurs, as it expanded into household items and tech.

The digital gig economy allows women to work on their own terms while balancing childcare or other family responsibilities. The growing demand for remote services has provided more income-generating opportunities for women, without the need for significant upfront capital investment. Women have increasingly been able to pursue work-from-home opportunities, especially during the COVID-19 pandemic, when **virtual assistant, social media management, and content creation roles became more common.**

In the last 10 years, the explosion of social media has given women new ways to earn income through **content creation and influencing**.

**Instagram and YouTube:** Women have built personal brands on platforms like Instagram and YouTube, where they create content related to beauty, fitness, parenting, and lifestyle. These influencers often collaborate with brands for sponsored content, making substantial incomes through digital marketing.

**Affiliate marketing:** Some women use affiliate marketing, where they promote products online and earn a commission on sales made through their referral links. This can be an additional income stream for those with an engaged online audience.

**Blogging and Vlogging** (video blogging): Blogging has become a full-time career for many women. Topics range from food, travel, lifestyle, fashion, and fitness to personal finance. Successful bloggers often monetise through advertisements, sponsored content, affiliate marketing, and by joining platform-based programmes like YouTube's Partner Program.

Social media has transformed from a personal space to a business opportunity for many women. With the ability to reach a global audience, women can now monetise their online presence, providing more opportunities for financial independence.

## 7.3 Shared economy and innovation

**Airbnb hosting:** Women have embraced platforms like Airbnb, turning their homes or spare rooms into short-term rental properties. This flexible model allows women to generate extra income by renting out their space, which has been particularly useful for stay-at-home mothers or women looking for part-time income.

**Home-based childcare:** Many women have set up home-based daycare centres to care for children in their communities. This allows them to combine earning an income with raising their own children.

**Virtual assistance:** As remote work continues to grow, many women have taken up virtual assistant roles, providing administrative support to businesses and entrepreneurs from home.

The world of women's income generation has shifted dramatically over the past 30 years, with women moving from informal, home-based direct sales and crafting to becoming global digital entrepreneurs, freelancers, and gig economy participants.

## 7.4 Financial barriers in the informal sector

While the informal sector offers opportunities for financial independence, **women continue to face significant barriers**:

- **Limited access to credit and capital:** Many women lack access to **business loans, credit facilities, and investment capital**, making it difficult to scale their businesses.
- **Legal and regulatory challenges:** Informal businesses often operate **without legal protection**, making them vulnerable to **evictions, fines, or exploitation**.
- **Lack of social protection:** Many women in informal work do not **contribute to pension funds, have formal contracts, or receive benefits**, leaving them financially vulnerable.
- **Gender-based discrimination:** Women entrepreneurs still face **biases and societal pressures**, limiting their ability to grow their businesses.

## 7.5 Building a sustainable future

Technology is **reshaping** the informal sector, giving women **new opportunities to generate income and expand their businesses.**

- **Mobile banking and digital payments:** Platforms such as **eWallet, SnapScan, and PayPal** enable women to **receive payments securely and manage their businesses more effectively.**
- **Social media and e-commerce:** Women entrepreneurs can now sell their products through **Facebook Marketplace, Instagram, WhatsApp Business, and Takealot**, reaching a wider audience.
- **Online learning and upskilling:** Platforms like **LinkedIn Learning, Udemy, and Coursera** provide women with **affordable skills training** in finance, marketing, and business management.

Governments and NGOs have increasingly recognised the **importance of supporting women entrepreneurs** in the informal sector. Initiatives, including

- **the Small Enterprise Development Agency,** which provides business support, training, and funding for small businesses;
- **the National Empowerment Fund**, which offers financial support to women-owned businesses; and

- programmes such as **Women in Business South Africa** and **Siyabonga Africa** provide mentorship and resources for female entrepreneurs.

While women have made significant strides in economic participation, there is still work to be done to eliminate barriers and ensure equal financial opportunities. Encouraging financial education, access to funding, and legal protections will help women transition from survival-based income generation to long-term financial security.

## 7.6 Key takeaways

- Women have historically played a major role in informal trade, adapting to economic and technological changes to create financial stability.
- Despite opportunities, financial barriers such as lack of credit, legal protection, and social security continue to limit women's business growth.
- Technology and digital platforms are empowering women, making it easier to start and grow businesses.
- Government programmes and NGO initiatives are helping to support women entrepreneurs in South Africa.
- Women must continue to seek education, resources, and financial planning strategies to secure their financial independence and success.

# PART III: RESEARCH AND PRACTICAL STRATEGIES

## Chapter 8: What Women Think – A Research-based Perspective

To understand the current situation and women's attitudes towards financial decision making and retirement investing in South Africa, an exploratory study was conducted in three phases. Drawing on qualitative research, the study focused on high-net-worth clients of a major JSE-listed financial services firm that provides comprehensive services (from fiduciary services, i.e. wills and trusts, to retirement and financial planning). The objective was to understand the current attitudes and behaviours of women when it comes to financial planning.

*Figure 8.1 Research design and data collection process*

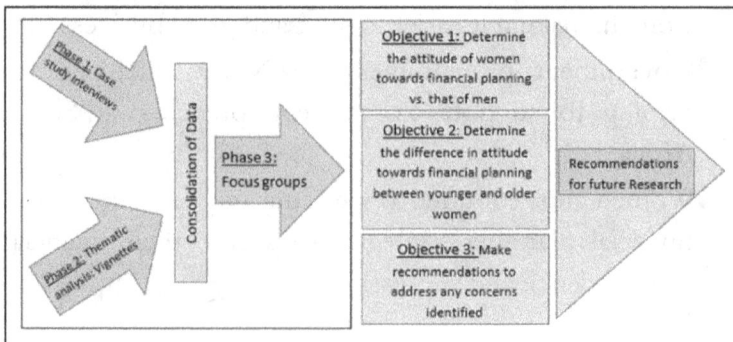

## 8.1 Phase 1: Semi-structured case-study interviews

The primary research was conducted through semi-structured one-on-one interviews with **20 financial advisers** within the financial services company and three industry experts to collect case information on gender- and age-specific attitudes towards financial decision making and identify potential interventions for women. Privacy was crucial, and participants discussed two to four cases they found most relevant.

Participants chose cases based on their typical clients' characteristics. The following questions were provided as context to prepare for the interviews:

1. Why was this case applicable to the research study?
2. Why did they require financial assistance or advice?
3. What did their planning structure look like before consulting the financial adviser?
4. What did their planning structure look like after consulting the financial adviser?
5. How could the outcomes of this scenario have been different?
6. Age, gender, marital status, dependents, working/not, qualified/not, updated will/not?
7. Own business, buy-and-sell contract for succession (if applicable)?
8. Group scheme benefits from employer, own

retirement annuity, own risk planning?

9. Own emergency fund?

Client details were anonymised to ensure their privacy was maintained. The feedback from the interviews conducted in phase 1 was used to develop the vignettes that served to encapsulate the key themes and were later used as discussion prompts in the focus groups.

In addition to the feedback, descriptive data were collected to clarify gender- and age-based differences in financial behaviours. The research underscores clear gender differences in financial planning behaviours and distinct differences between younger and older women in terms of their financial planning behaviours.

Table 8.1 reveals that, of the 65 cases, two-thirds were over the age of 45, and most were women. Among those who had worked at some stage in their life (of which women were the majority), only 35% had contributed to a group retirement fund. Within that group, women were far more likely to do so. This suggests that women are more likely to make provision for retirement if it is a compulsory benefit at a company.

Just over half of those with emergency funds were women, and nearly nine out of ten cases had been married, with just over two-thirds of these being women as well. The majority of marriages were under antenuptial contracts (ANCs), again with women making up the larger share, underlining the risks they face if they do not make financial provision in their own names, particularly in cases of divorce or unforeseen death of a spouse.

*Table 8.1 Demographic and financial characteristics of 65 cases discussed during structured one-on-one interviews, disaggregated by gender.*

| Variable | Total sample | Women | Men |
|---|---|---|---|
| Older than 45 years | 66% (43/65) | 67% (29/43) | 33% (14/43) |
| Worked at some stage | 72% (47/65) | 60% (28/47) | 40% (19/47) |
| Contributed to a group retirement fund | 35% (23/65) | 83% (19/23) | 17% (4/23) |
| Had emergency funds | 57% (37/65) | 54% (20/37) | 46% (17/37) |
| Married at some stage | 89% (58/65) | 67% (39/58) | 33% (19/58) |
| Married by antenuptial contract | 68% (44/65) | 64% (28/44) | 36% (16/44) |
| Had a will | 68% (44/65) | 70% (31/44) | 30% (13/44) |
| Used trusts | 14% (9/65) | 33% (3/9) | 67% (6/9) |

**Note:** *Antenuptial contract refers to a marriage contract that dictates the terms of property ownership and financial management between spouses.*

Encouragingly, of those who had wills in place, 70% were women, indicating that they considered it an important financial instrument. Despite many women having wills, they are often unsure of the validity and feasibility of their wills after restructuring to trust structures and do not test the liquidity and validity of the will, seeking assistance from a financial adviser only after an event occurs. In this sample, 67% of men made use of trusts compared to 33% of women. This implies that more men are making use of professional services, such as financial advisers, legal services, and tax consultants.

Age-related trends (Table 8.2) reveal that of the 45 women in the sample, 29 were older than 45 years, as were 14 of the 20 men. Nearly nine out of ten participants had been married at some point, and again, most of them were older than 45. Among those married under ANC (68% of the group), 70% were over 45. This underscores the importance of making provision in one's own name in case of unforeseen events, such as divorce or the death of a spouse.

Estate planning also showed an age trend: 77% of those with wills were over 45, suggesting that younger individuals may be less likely to plan for eventualities. Only a small proportion made use of trusts, but almost all of those were over the age of 45, indicating that older individuals consider this instrument important for protecting and transferring assets to the next generation or as an efficient tax structure.

Similarly, of those who contributed to a group retirement fund, 57% were over the age of 45, suggesting that older people are more likely to make provision for retirement when contributions are compulsory. Just over half of the cases made provision for emergency funds, and most of them were over 45, while younger individuals in this sample seemed less concerned about an emergency fund.

*Table 8.2 Demographic and financial characteristics of 65 cases discussed during structured one-on-one interviews, disaggregated by age.*

| Variable | Total sample | < 45 years | ≥ 45 years |
|---|---|---|---|
| Men | 31% (20/65) | 30% (6/20) | 70% (14/20) |
| Women | 69% (45/65) | 36% (16/45) | 64% (29/45) |
| Divorced, married, widow/er | 89% (58/65) | 29% (17/58) | 71% (41/58) |
| Antenuptial contract | 68% (44/65) | 30% (13/44) | 70% (31/44) |
| Will | 68% (44/65) | 23% (10/44) | 77% (34/44) |
| Trust | 14% (9/65) | 11% (1/9) | 89% (8/9) |
| Group retirement fund | 35% (23/65) | 43% (10/23) | 57% (13/23) |
| Emergency fund | 57% (37/65) | 27% (10/37) | 73% (27/37) |

**Note:** *Antenuptial contract refers to a marriage contract that dictates the terms of property ownership and financial management between spouses.*

Table 8.3 summarises the demographic and financial characteristics of the female cases in the study. In the sample, nearly two-thirds of the women were over the age of 45. Among those who contributed to a group retirement fund 58% were over the age of 45, indicating that women over 45 are generally more concerned about retirement planning than younger women. Women under 45 made up only one-quarter of those with an emergency fund. This suggests that younger women in this sample did not prioritise having an emergency fund, showing a lack of planning for unexpected financial eventualities.

*Table 8.3 Demographic and financial characteristics of 45 female cases discussed during structured one-on-one interviews*

| Variable | < 45 years | ≥ 45 years |
| --- | --- | --- |
| Women | 36% (16/45) | 64% (29/45) |
| Divorced, married, widow | 28% (11/39) | 72% (28/39) |
| Will | 23% (7/31) | 77% (24/31) |
| Trust | 33% (1/3) | 67% (2/3) |
| Group retirement fund | 42% (8/19) | 58% (11/19) |
| Emergency fund | 25% (5/20) | 75% (15/20) |

Only three women in the study made use of trusts, and two of those were older than 45, suggesting that older women were more likely to protect their assets and ensure

112

transferability to the next generation using trusts.

Additionally, among the 31 who had a will, only seven were younger than 45, which may imply that, in this sample, younger women did not plan sufficiently for eventualities such as death or incapacitation.

Based on a more in-depth review of the data, cases were grouped into two main categories: those who were well informed about financial planning matters and those who were unaware of the consequences of a lack of planning (Table 8.4). We can see that a large portion (58%) of the participants were completely unaware of the consequences of lack of planning in Table 8.4.

Table 8.4 Level of understanding of financial planning among 65 cases discussed during structured one-on-one interviews

|  | Total | 25–44 years | | ≥ 45 years | |
|---|---|---|---|---|---|
|  |  | Men | Women | Men | Women |
| Well informed about financial planning matters | 27 | 4 | 7 | 7 | 9 |
| Unaware of consequences associated with a lack of planning | 38 | 2 | 9 | 7 | 20 |
| **Total** | **65** | **6** | **16** | **14** | **29** |

Less than half of this sample were well informed on financial matters, while nearly two-thirds were unaware of the consequences of a lack of planning, highlighting a clear gap in financial literacy. Among those who were informed, women made up 59%, but within the uninformed group, women were the majority, at 76%. This suggests that women in this sample were less financially literate than men. Notably, most of these uninformed women were 45 or older, suggesting that older women, in particular, were less financially literate than their younger counterparts.

## 8.2 Phase 2: Vignettes

A vignette is a short, impressionistic piece that presents a hypothetical situation, focusing on a social norm, character, idea, or object (Charmaz, 2000). Insights from the interviews were distilled into six short narrative scenarios reflecting varying attitudes and practices in financial planning.

1. **Reliance on spouse:** Many women depended entirely on their partners for financial decisions, which often left them unprepared when unexpected events (like death or divorce) occurred.
2. **Lack of involvement:** A significant number of women were not engaged in the financial planning process, remaining unaware of the broader financial picture or the implications of trust structures.
3. **Disinterest or low motivation:** Some participants

showed a general lack of interest in long-term financial planning, preferring to focus on immediate needs until a crisis forced them to act.

4. **Bearing the cost of a big-spending spouse:** In a few cases, the financial burden imposed by a partner's extravagant spending delayed or disrupted retirement planning.

5. **Taking charge:** Some of the participants were proactive, managing their own finances with a high level of literacy and preparedness, with most setting up emergency funds and valid wills.

6. **Home-based financial education:** A small segment credited their financial awareness to lessons learned at home, usually through parental influence.

The thematic analysis of the vignettes involved an iterative process aimed at progressively deepening our understanding of the financial attitudes and behaviours of the participants. Each repetition of the analysis brought us closer to uncovering significant patterns, with different variables being measured in each vignette. The sample of 65 cases (20 male and 45 female) was **grouped into specific themes.**

1. **My spouse will provide** (25 cases)
2. **I'm not involved in financial planning decisions** (9 cases)
3. **I'm not interested, not motivated enough** (5 cases)
4. **Carrying the cost of my spouse – *'big spender'*** (4 cases)
5. **Making my own financial planning decisions** (16 cases)
6. **Educated at home on financial planning matters** (6

cases)

---

---

Each vignette represents the cases linked to a particular theme, supported by **verbatim quotes reflecting the participants' views:**

## *Theme 1: My spouse will provide (25)*

This code was used when a person relied completely on a spouse to make provision for their retirement, everyday needs, and in the event of something unforeseen taking place. This parent code denotes the elements relating to the typical middle-class man or woman who wants to provide quality of life to his/her family by making provision for their everyday needs and providing a stable environment for their children to excel at school and their spouse to excel in their career or business.

*Johan and Louise both had diploma-level academic qualifications. Louise worked until the children were born, and then became a housewife, while Johan provided an allowance for her to run the household (which was never enough), as in this way, he could control her spending. He did not really want her to work and be self-sufficient, but rather to be dependent on him. No planning was done in her name. She was not involved in the finances at all, though he had some risk*

116

*cover and discretionary and retirement savings in place, in his name. Johan died and left her with no knowledge of their financial situation, what her future income needs were, and how to budget and make provision for retirement. She had to care for her underage children and was devastated.*

The following verbatim quotations reflect the participants' views regarding *my spouse will provide*:

| . . . Since he is the breadwinner, no planning is needed in my name | ... this is his second marriage. Since his ex has re-married, she will not be involved if something unforseen happens | ... we only have some assets, house and car and do not need a valid will. |
| --- | --- | --- |

Of this group of **25 cases**, 76% (19/25) were in need of financial advice after an eventuality had taken place, i.e. the death of a spouse, serious illness, or divorce. Seventy-one per cent of the male cases (5/7) needed holistic financial advice, including drawing up a will or setting up a trust. This may imply that they plan long term and do not wait for an eventuality to take place, in contrast with 94% (17/18) of the female cases. In 44% (11/25) of these cases, they had no valid will, or the liquidity of the will was not sufficient to provide as planned. Only in 32% (8/25) of these cases did they have emergency funds, which implies that they would have been destitute in the event of any eventuality occuring, due to their lack of planning. Only 25% (2/8) of all those who had emergency funds in this group were women, of whom 50% (1/2) were over the age of 45. Of this group,

117

56% (14/25) had wills drafted and assumed that their affairs were in order.

## Theme 2: I'm not involved in financial planning decisions (9)

This code was used when a person was not involved in making any financial decisions and was unaware of the consequences of not making provision in his or her own name, especially in the event of death, divorce, or disability/dreaded disease of self or spouse. In many of these cases, trust structures, farms, or their own businesses were involved.

**Samuel and Mavis:** *Mavis was a qualified nurse, and Samuel managed the family farm that he had inherited from his father. This was his second marriage, and he had two boys from a previous marriage. The family was rather wealthy, and Mavis used his credit card (which he monitored on his phone) for all expenses. She did not work according to a budget. She had no idea about their financial position, and he controlled both their spending habits. No provision or planning was done in her name. All assets (including his inheritance) were moved into a trust for the next generation. She was an income beneficiary of the trust. Samuel died and left her with no knowledge of their financial situation or the trust, their medical aid, and what their household expenses came to, monthly. She had no assets and no provision for retirement, and was dependent on the children, as the trust was under their control as trustees.*

The following quotations reflect the participants' views regarding *I'm not involved in financial planning decisions.*

... I am married COP, and, thus, will be taken care of in the event of death or divorce...

... we are paying policies on my husband's name, thus, I will be taken care of...

... I am working for my husband in the business; he pays policies, taken out in my name...

Of the above **9 cases**, 89% involved women, of which 63% (5/8) were over the age of 45. In 50% (4/8) of the cases involving women, trusts were in place. Since the women were not involved in any financial decisions, the 63% (5/8) that did have wills in place could not understand why their spouses' wishes could not be honoured, though the circumstances were caused by loan accounts to/from the trusts and lack of liquidity in the estate. In 100% of the cases involving women, they sought financial advice only after an eventuality had taken place, i.e. divorce or serious illness/death of the spouse, implying that the women in these cases did not make financial decisions or plan for retirement prior to the events. In some instances, the trust was the beneficiary of the policy on the life of the spouses, which did not provide liquidity in the estate. The women married in community of property in the above cases (3/8, 38%) were also unaware of the consequences of not making provision in their own names. Their right to 50% of the estate community of property had deteriorated, due to the transfer of assets over time to the trust, without provision being made for liquidity and without them being involved in the trust. Of the women, 75% (6/8) had no emergency funds. We can infer that women are oblivious to the consequences, due to their lack of financial literacy and not being involved in financial planning decisions, as they believe that it is traditionally the responsibility of the man to provide.

### Theme 3: I'm not interested, not motivated enough (5)

> This code was used when a person was not interested or motivated to make any financial decisions, as he or she was comfortable with the current situation. They lived for the present and were scared to face reality, as it would mean that they would have to make financial decisions. They might only act when an eventuality took place.

***David and Francis:*** *He ran a successful business as a developer, but did not always have enough cash flow. Francis had a hobby that provided ad-hoc income. They were both intelligent, had a nice house, enjoyed spectacular holidays, and the good life. He wanted to protect her from the stress related to their cash flow that came under pressure from time to time, and, thus, did not share information on their situation. He died suddenly in a car accident, and she had no knowledge of how to run the business, which was needed to provide for her future needs and those of the children.*

The following quotations reflect the participants' views regarding ***I'm not interested, not motivated enough.***

> ... I do not have to understand where the contracts for my husband's business are coming from ...

> ... we live in the 'now' and do not need to plan for old age, as we are still young ...

> ... we do not have it 'thin' financially; thus, we do not have to plan for retirement, prospective inheritance will provide ...

Of the **5 cases** above, 60% were women, of whom 67% (2/3) were over the age of 45. Moreover, 67% of these women (2/3) sought advice only after the eventuality took place, regarding delayed investing, since they had no financial planning in their own name, and policies had lapsed when they got divorced. They were all working women, of whom 67% (2/3) were divorced after having been married in community of property. The men (40%) had no will in place, but 100% had emergency funds. The men all sought financial advice regarding options in lump-sum investment.

## Theme 4: Carrying the cost of my spouse—big spender (4)

This code was used when a person was expected to pay the expenses of a spouse who did not budget or plan, requiring the use of their emergency funds, which delayed retirement planning.

*Fikile and Constance: He was a building contractor, managing his own business that relied on contracts from the municipality. Constance was a store manager and earned a steady income, with bonus incentives from time to time. She would save the bonuses in an account for emergency funds, held at a financial institution, but due to Fekile's spending habits (including his spending on her), she had no control over the deployment of her monthly income or bonuses, as they were always needed to cover expenses in the short term, while he was awaiting new contracts. He had no long-term outlook and always waited for 'the next big one' to materialise. Constance could not make provision for the future, as their high standard of living absorbed all her potential savings.*

The following quotations reflect the participants' views regarding **Carrying the cost of my spouse—big spender**.

... although we are using money from my emergency funds, we will replace it when the next contract comes in ...

... our farming income and expenses are sporadic; we will save after we paid expenses ...

... my second husband's business venture ate into my emergency fund [divorce settlement]. He will repay me once it is 'up and running' ...

Half of the **4 cases** were women, and three-quarters of the group were married by ANC. Though they were all working, none made any contribution to a group retirement fund (which implies that they needed all their income monthly, and did not see the need to plan for retirement), although all cases had an emergency fund in place. We can infer from the cases that all wanted to save after they had paid all their expenses and those of their spouses, but did not budget or set goals for the long term. Some were married to controlling men and were unaware of the consequences of a lack of planning in their own name, and that they would not be able to replace the emergency funds if there was no specific budget in place, or goals set.

## Theme 5: Making my own financial planning decisions (16)

> This code was used when a person made provision in their own name, made decisions on financial planning, and considered themself financially literate.

*Keith and Robin: Keith sold his business when he retired early, at 55. His wife, Robin, was then aged 50. She had 17 years' service at a consultancy firm, and had saved monthly from her very first paycheck as the human resources manager. She had educated herself on different financial options at an early age. She invested two-thirds of the capital at her early retirement into a linked annuity. Her financial adviser had planned for the short, medium, and long term, and an emergency fund was created. Keith applied for tax amnesty some years earlier and had offshore and local trusts, into which he bought different properties. Their children were well qualified and lived overseas. Robin was also a trustee and provided input at the annual trustee meetings with their financial adviser.*

The following quotations reflect the participants' views regarding **making my own financial planning decisions**.

... I do not ever want to be dependent on anyone, and need a financial plan ...

... my mother was a single parent, and I know that you can only depend on yourself for retirement ...

... my adviser introduced some financial concepts and a plan, and kept me on track with annual reviews ...

Of the **16 cases** above, 38% (6/16) were men. Among the men, 83% (5/6) were over the age of 45; all were married by ANC, made use of a trust, and had a valid will.

Two-thirds were retired, and 83% (5/6) had emergency funds. In contrast, 62% were women, of whom 60% (6/10) were over the age of 45. All the women in these cases had a valid will and emergency funds, 20% (2/10) were retired or retrenched, and only 10% (1/10) did not contribute to their own group retirement fund. Only 20% (2/10) were single; the other 80% (8/10) were married by ANC, of which 25% (2/8) had since divorced. These women used no trusts, and it could be inferred from the cases that these women did not make use of tax professionals. They were, however, quite astute regarding financial planning and thus had a high level of financial literacy. Some pointed out that they had become aware of financial planning matters after a parent died, or they got divorced, or after having acquired the services of a financial adviser.

## Theme 6: Educated at home on financial planning matters (6)

This code was used when a participant was first educated on financial planning matters by their parents.

***Ciska and Eloise:*** *Ciska's ex-husband committed suicide, and she inherited a lump sum from life policies and a large pension fund, since he had been in the police force. She invested the money through a financial adviser and built a rather large share portfolio. She also had* *policies in her own name. She had been living with Eloise (her life partner) for the past six years, who was also self-sufficient as an engineer and had a retirement plan. Eloise owned a property in Hermanus, where they planned to retire in a few years. Eloise was not entirely sure that she was getting the best returns on her investments and wanted to review the fund performances and fees with her adviser. Ciska wanted to make changes to her will and update the beneficiary nominations on her policies.*

The following quotations reflect the participants' views regarding **educated at home on financial planning matters**.

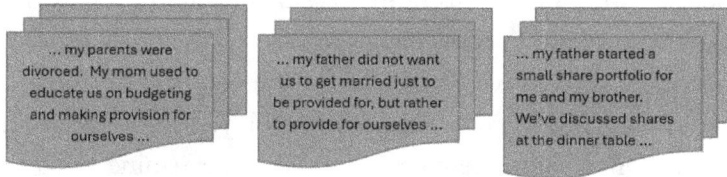

| ... my parents were divorced. My mom used to educate us on budgeting and making provision for ourselves ... | ... my father did not want us to get married just to be provided for, but rather to provide for ourselves ... | ... my father started a small share portfolio for me and my brother. We've discussed shares at the dinner table ... |
|---|---|---|

Of the **6 cases** above, 67% (4/6) were women, of whom 50% (2/4) were over the age of 45. All the women were working, and 75% contributed to a group retirement fund, while 50% (2/4) had emergency funds and a valid will. Three-quarters of the women were single, and 25% were divorced, though previously married by ANC. It can be inferred that, after first being introduced to financial matters and concepts in their parents' home, these cases feared being dependent on anyone else. They took responsibility for educating themselves and making their own financial decisions. In the above cases, 33% (2/6) of males were both under the age of 45 and married by ANC. They were

125

working and contributed to group retirement funds.

They also had emergency funds available, though only 50% had a valid will. Even the men sought financial advice, as they considered themselves financially literate and wanted to make use of financial advisers. Their first exposure to financial planning concepts was at home, with parents who worked in a bank, other financial institution, or in their own business.

## 8.3 Phase 3: Focus groups

Two focus groups (comprising nine and ten women each) met in structured two-hour sessions (Figure 8.2). The vignettes were presented along with background information to provide context for the research objectives. The nominal group technique was employed to validate and expand on the interview findings and to determine areas of focus or 'next best actions'.

The questions asked were

1. What is holding women back from fully participating in the economy and making financial decisions?
2. How can we create awareness to address these issues and bring women to action?
3. What advice would you give your *'younger self'* regarding taking responsibility for your own financial future?

*Figure 8.2   10 October 2017 focus groups 1 (top; morning) and 2 (bottom; afternoon)*

The focus group results that can be seen in Table 8.5, highlight clear priorities across the three questions. For barriers to women's full participation in the economy, the traditional role of women was ranked as the biggest obstacle, followed by lack of financial literacy and low self-confidence, while the absence of a trusted adviser was seen as the least important. In terms of creating awareness, the top strategies identified were partnerships that demonstrate tangible benefits and awareness campaigns, with education at home also considered valuable. Finally, when asked what advice they would give their younger selves, participants emphasised the importance of educating themselves and saving for retirement, while ensuring a valid will was also noted. Across all age groups, budget control and seeking professional advice ranked lower, suggesting women valued empowerment through knowledge and proactive planning over external support

*Table 8.5. Ranked responses of 19 female participants during the focus group sessions. (1 being most likely, 5 being least likely)*

| | Group 1 | Group 2 | Overall | < 45 years | ≥ 45 years |
|---|---|---|---|---|---|
| **Question 1:** What is holding women back from fully participating in the economy and making financial decisions? | | | | | |
| **Responses** | | | | | |
| A. Traditional role of women | 2 | 2 | 1 | 1 | 1 |
| B. Lack of self-confidence | 3 | 4 | 3 | 3 | 3 |
| C. Controlling men | 4 | 5 | 4 | 4 | 4 |
| D. Not financially literate | 1 | 3 | 2 | 2 | 2 |
| E. Lack of a trusted adviser | 5 | 5 | 5 | 5 | 5 |

**Question 2:** How can we create awareness to address these issues and bring women to action?

**Responses**

| | | | | | | |
|---|---|---|---|---|---|---|
| A. | Educate at home | 3 | 4 | 3 | 2 | 3 |
| B. | Fiduciary responsibility | 5 | 2 | 4 | 4 | 5 |
| C. | Trusted adviser | 4 | 5 | 5 | 5 | 4 |
| D. | Partnership (benefits) | 1 | 1 | 1 | 1 | 1 |
| E. | Awareness campaigns | 2 | 3 | 2 | 3 | 2 |

**Question 3:** What advice would you give your 'younger self' regarding taking responsibility for your own financial future?

**Responses**

| | | | | | | |
|---|---|---|---|---|---|---|
| A. | Valid will | 2 | 3 | 3 | 3 | 3 |
| B. | Saving for retirement | 3 | 1 | 2 | 1 | 2 |
| C. | Educate yourself | 1 | 2 | 1 | 2 | 1 |
| D. | Budget control | 4 | 4 | 4 | 4 | 4 |
| E. | Professional advice | 5 | 5 | 5 | 5 | 5 |

## 8.4 Discussion

This study explored how women in South Africa approach financial decision making and retirement investing. Unexpected events, such as the loss of a spouse or a sudden illness, can have a devastating impact if you're not financially prepared. We found that women often only act after such events occur, highlighting a need for better planning and preparedness. It highlights the need for improved financial literacy among women and suggests that empowering them with tailored advice and greater involvement in decision making can help secure a more stable financial future. Emergency funds, wills, and trust structures are essential tools in safeguarding your financial future. Yet, our data shows that many women lack these critical safety nets. By prioritising these elements in your financial plan, you can ensure that you're protected no matter what life throws your way.

## 8.5 Key takeaways

### *Significant gender gap in financial behaviour*

- Women in the sample show less engagement in proactive financial planning compared to men.
- Retirement planning is often passive—relying mainly on employer-mandated group retirement funds.
- Use of professional services (financial advisers, tax consultants, legal experts) is much lower among women.

## Limited understanding of key financial tools
- While women often use wills, there is a limited understanding of liquidity needs for proper execution.
- Many women agree to ANCs without grasping the financial consequences.
- Emergency fund usage is notably lower among women, showing reactive rather than proactive planning.

## Age matters: Different attitudes across generations
- Women over 45 are less financially literate than their younger counterparts.
- Older women made more use of emergency funds and trust structures but generally had less knowledge.
- Younger women prioritise education, independence, and shared responsibility in financial matters.

## Low financial literacy = low confidence
- Many women still feel underqualified to manage money due to societal conditioning and historical exclusion.
- There's a continued dependence on male partners for financial decisions—even among educated women.
- Financial literacy and professional advice are *complementary*, not interchangeable.

## Advice often comes too late
- Women tend to seek financial advice **after** a crisis (death, divorce), rather than as a preventive measure.
- Lack of **trusted financial advisers** is a key barrier to early financial engagement.

- Women are open to advice—but need better access, transparency, and trust in advisory services.

## *Holistic, gender-sensitive advice is essential*

- Financial, legal, and tax professionals must offer **comprehensive**, not one-off, advice.
- Planning must include:
    - Liquidity considerations for executing wills and trust structures.
    - Regular updates to beneficiaries and nominees.
    - Joint tax planning and equal use of rebates by both spouses.
    - Protection for business owners and their families in the case of death or disability.

## *Financial empowerment benefits everyone*

- Women's financial security positively impacts families, communities, and the broader economy.
- Encouraging women to plan, invest, and save ensures they don't outlive their income sources.
- Tax policies and exemptions should support individual financial autonomy within partnerships.

As I've come to learn, financial empowerment isn't just about access to resources—it's about building understanding, nurturing confidence, and providing consistent support.

# Chapter 9: Steps to Achieving Financial Independence

This chapter emphasises the transformative role that financial literacy plays in planning for retirement and making sound financial decisions. It urges you to reflect on your own financial status and consider areas where you can take greater control. The chapter outlines practical steps that can empower you to move toward financial independence. Here are some practical steps to becoming financially independent.

## 9.1 Understanding your marriage regime

**Legal framework:** In South Africa, the type of marriage you enter into (civil, civil union, customary, and soon possibly religious) influences the financial and legal implications of your union. The Matrimonial Property Act (No. 88 of 1984) outlines three main regimes:

- **Marriage in community of property**
- **Marriage out of community of property without accrual**, also known as ANC without accrual
- **Marriage out of community of property with accrual,** also known as ANC with accrual

The characteristics of each of these marriage regimes are detailed in Tables 9.1 and 9.2.

**Financial impact:** Knowing your marriage regime helps you understand asset ownership, financial responsibilities, and tax implications. Women who are better informed tend to make stronger investment decisions, evidenced by having emergency funds, valid wills, and diversified portfolios.

*Table 9.1 Characteristics of the marriage in community of property regime*

| Aspect | Marriage in community of property |
|---|---|
| Definition | Default regime if no antenuptial agreement is signed. Both spouses' assets and liabilities combine into one joint estate. |
| Asset ownership | Assets owned before the marriage and acquired during the marriage are jointly owned (50% ownership each). |
| Liabilities | Both spouses are equally liable for debts incurred during the marriage. |
| Consent for transactions | Written consent is required for certain transactions, such as selling immovable property or signing surety agreements. |
| Impact of insolvency | If one spouse is declared insolvent, the joint estate is sequestrated, and both spouses are affected. |
| Advantages | Protects the non-earning spouse (traditionally the wife) by ensuring 50% ownership of the joint estate. |
| Disadvantages | Both spouses are liable for each other's debts, and financial independence is limited due to shared ownership of assets. |
| Ideal for | Couples who are comfortable sharing all assets and liabilities equally. |

*Table 9.2 Characteristics of the marriage out of community of property with/without accrual regimes*

| Key features | Advantages | Disadvantages |
|---|---|---|
| **Marriage out of community of property without accrual** | | |
| Requires an antenuptial agreement signed before marriage. | Each spouse retains separate estates, protecting their assets from the other's debts. | No sharing of assets or liabilities, which may lead to financial inequality if one spouse earns less. |
| No sharing of assets or debts; each spouse is solely responsible for their own finances. | Spouses are free to manage their finances and business dealings independently. | Upon divorce, one spouse may leave the marriage with no claim to the other's estate. |
| At divorce or death, no claim exists on the other spouse's estate (except for maintenance, if applicable). | Protects assets acquired before and during the marriage. | Requires careful financial planning to ensure fairness if one spouse contributes more to the household. |
| **Marriage out of community of property with accrual system** | | |
| Requires an ANC with accrual specified. | Provides fairness by allowing the spouse with the smaller accrual to claim 50% of the growth difference. | Requires clear record-keeping and calculation of starting and accrued values for each spouse's estate. |

135

| | | |
|---|---|---|
| Each spouse retains their separate estate during the marriage. | Protects assets from creditors of the other spouse during the marriage. | Accrual claims are only realisable upon divorce or death, not during the marriage. |
| At dissolution of marriage, the spouse with lesser growth in their estate can claim from the other spouse. | Fair to spouses who contribute non-financially to the marriage, e.g. childcare or homemaking. | Complex to implement and requires professional assistance for calculation and drafting ANC. |

By taking the time to educate yourself and seek out reliable information, you can build a robust investment strategy that aligns with your goals.

## 9.2 Creating and managing a budget

- **Track income and expenses:** Utilise spreadsheets or budgeting apps to keep detailed records of your earnings and outgoings.
- **Set and pursue financial goals:** Define both short-term and long-term objectives and develop a structured plan to achieve them.
- **Regular reviews:** Consistently revisit and adjust your budget to ensure you're on track, with clear sections for income, fixed and variable expenses, savings goals, and a final summary showing your remaining balance.

# How to use the budget template below (Table 9.3)

1.  **Income section**: Record all sources of income for the month. Include your salary, any freelance or side income, and other earnings such as investment returns.
2.  **Fixed expenses**: These are regular monthly costs that typically don't change, like rent or bond payments, utility bills, and debt repayments.
3.  **Variable expenses**: Track spending on items that vary month-to-month, such as groceries, dining out, and transport.
4.  **Savings goals**: Allocate amounts towards specific savings goals like an emergency fund, retirement, or education.
5.  **Summary**: At the end of the month, calculate your total income, expenses, and savings. The *remaining balance* reflects what's left after expenses and savings.

*Table 9.3 Budget template*

| Category | Planned | Actual amount | Difference |
|---|---|---|---|
| **Income** <br> Salary <br> Freelance/side income <br> Investments <br> Other income | | | |
| **Total income** | | | |
| **Fixed expenses** <br> Rent/bond | | | |

| | | | |
|---|---|---|---|
| Utilities (water, electricity, rates, taxes) | | | |
| Internet and phone | | | |
| Insurance (health, life, short-term) | | | |
| Debt repayments (loan, credit card) | | | |
| Savings/investments | | | |
| Other fixed expenses | | | |
| **Total fixed expenses** | | | |
| **Variable expenses** | | | |
| Groceries | | | |
| Eating out/entertainment | | | |
| Transport (fuel, etc.) | | | |
| Personal care (clothing, etc.) | | | |
| Healthcare | | | |
| Gifts/charity | | | |
| Miscellaneous | | | |
| **Total variable expenses** | | | |
| **Savings** | | | |
| Emergency fund | | | |
| Retirement fund | | | |
| Holiday fund | | | |
| Education fund | | | |
| Other savings | | | |
| **Total savings** | | | |
| **Summary** | | | |
| Total income | | | |

| | | | |
|---|---|---|---|
| Total fixed expenses | | | |
| Total variable expenses | | | |
| Total savings | | | |
| **Remaining balance** | | | |

## 9.3 Starting short-term saving and long-term investing

**Effective resource management:** Financial resilience is less about the size of your income and more about how you manage and optimise your resources, i.e. salary or income from a business.

**Flexible banking solutions:** Access to modern, **flexible banking services** can empower you to make informed and timely financial decisions. Women deserve to be rewarded for the positive financial strides they make, with benefits that honour their commitment to wellbeing. Banks offer savings accounts, loans, credit cards, tax-free investments, home loans, and numerous other products and services. You need a bank account that will allow you to save in different pockets, for different goals, while taking all these savings into account to improve your interest rates.

**Diverse investment options:** Consider a **mix of investments** such as bank investments, share portfolios, bonds, unit trusts, and retirement options. Diversifying both locally and globally can help manage risk and maximise returns.

**Emergency fund:** Aim to build an emergency fund covering **three to six months** of living expenses, ensuring that you have a financial buffer for unforeseen circumstances.

## 9.4 Planning for retirement and protection

**Retirement planning–assessing your needs:** Estimate the retirement **savings needed**—often 10 to 15 times your annual income—to maintain your desired lifestyle. Decide your **retirement age** based on your contributions: contributing more can let you retire earlier, while contributing less might mean a later retirement age.

**Contributions and adjustments:** Benefit from **tax deductions** on regular contributions, including employer-matched funds if available. The retirement plan encourages ad-hoc contributions when extra funds arise, with periodic reviews to adjust savings, retirement age, or investment strategies in response to changes like salary increases or bonuses.

## 9.5 Risk protection through life insurance

**Essential coverage:** Life insurance provides financial security for dependents by covering daily living expenses, debt obligations, and final expenses. This protection ensures that in the event of your death, your family isn't burdened with outstanding debts or unexpected costs.

**Offshore life insurance:** Considering US dollar-denominated policies can protect against local currency volatility, making it especially useful if you have international financial obligations, such as funding children's education or managing a foreign mortgage. Even if you have no obligations globally but have children working and living overseas and want to leave a legacy, you can take out offshore cover that is very tax efficient.

**Business obligations:** Business assurance should be addressed separately. You need to assure against all risks in the business if death or disability occurs. This will ensure that the business, or your share in it, will be sold for an appropriate/pre-determined price. By doing so, your family will not be left with the burden of an unrealised or bankrupt estate caused by prolonged succession or debts owed to creditors, which would otherwise fall on your personal estate.

## 9.6 Protecting your income and managing health risks

**Income protection:** Ensuring your income is secured is critical since it fuels your financial plan. Without a steady income, even the best savings strategies can falter.

**Severe illness benefits:** These benefits act as a safety net if you're diagnosed with a serious illness. They provide

- **income replacement:** Ensuring you can cover expenses during recovery.
- **medical and ancillary costs:** Helping manage expenses that standard health insurance might not cover, such as specialised treatments or home adaptations.
- **household support and rehabilitation:** Offering financial flexibility to maintain your household during difficult times. Some serious illnesses may require modifications to your home, such as installing ramps, handrails, or other accessibility aids.

**Education protection:** This can also be taken in local or global cover, to fund your children's education needs if you are unable to do so due to illness, disability, or death.

**Health insurance and medical aid:** Comprehensive health coverage prevents catastrophic out-of-pocket expenses, ensures access to quality care, and often includes preventive services. This not only supports immediate health needs but also contributes to long-term financial stability by reducing the risk of depleting savings for unexpected medical costs. Knowing that health expenses are covered provides peace of mind, reducing the mental and emotional stress often associated with potential financial burdens. This stability positively impacts overall wellbeing, creating a healthier foundation for making sound financial decisions.

## 9.7 Estate planning and leaving a legacy

**Planning your legacy through wills and trusts:** Secure your family's future through estate planning. Life cover can help offset estate taxes and other legal fees, ensuring that your heirs receive your assets as intended. You need to consult with an adviser who can calculate your obligations, asset value, and liquidity, after taking your marriage regime into account. Maintain a signed and valid, executable will and consider alternative structures like trusts for long-term asset protection.

There are several specific products that can insure against the costs incurred in the event of your death. Will drafting services are mostly free at most institutions and through corporate insurers, contracted to financial advisers.

**Essential documents for financial security:** This section highlights the importance of having all the necessary documents in place to safeguard your financial future and ensure smooth estate administration. It introduces a resource developed by Nikky Bush, who shares her personal experience on how a simple six-minute tragedy transformed her financial security.

- **Checklist:** Nikky's resource is a detailed file that lists the essential documents required for different scenarios. These documents are crucial for an adviser or executor to effectively manage and administer your estate.

- **Personal story:** The resource is grounded in Nikky's own journey, demonstrating the real-life impact of having these documents organised and accessible.

- **Virtual resource:** It's important to note that this is a virtual list available online, and it requires payment. For more details, you can visit the resource at https://nikkibush.com/product/what-if-file-pdf/

## 9.8 Engaging with financial advisers and services

**Overcoming hesitation:** Many women are often reluctant to seek professional financial advice due to mistrust or the intimidation of complex financial language. This reluctance usually leads to reactive decision making—seeking help only after life-altering events like divorce or the loss of a spouse.

**Proactive approach:** By consulting financial advisers before a crisis occurs, you can avoid pitfalls and develop a more confident, forward-thinking financial strategy.

**Find an adviser:** we are linked to a number of advisers in all areas, reach out today!

9.9 Key takeaways

1. **Know Your Marriage Regime and Its Financial Impact**

   Understanding your marital contract—whether in or out of community of property, with or without accrual—affects ownership of assets, debt responsibilities, tax implications, and estate planning. Educated women make stronger, more informed financial decisions.

2. **Create and Maintain a Realistic Budget**

   Budgeting is foundational to financial independence. Track your income, fixed and variable expenses, and savings. Regularly review your budget to stay on course and identify areas for improvement.

3. **Start Saving and Investing Early**

   Financial independence is not just about income—it's about how effectively you manage it. Build short-term savings for emergencies and long-term investments for retirement and wealth creation. Diversify investments to manage risk.

4. **Plan Proactively for Retirement**

   Estimate how much you need for a comfortable retirement—often 10 to 15 times your annual income. Adjust your contributions over time and take advantage of tax deductions and employer contributions where possible.

5. **Protect Yourself and Your Family with Insurance**

   Life insurance ensures your dependents aren't left with

debt or financial uncertainty. Offshore life policies and business assurance can provide added protection and legacy planning, especially in complex family or business situations.

6. **Safeguard Your Income and Health**
   Income protection and severe illness cover act as financial lifelines during unexpected health crises. These policies help maintain your lifestyle and household stability during recovery and beyond.

7. **Ensure Access to Quality Healthcare**
   Medical aid and health insurance reduce the risk of depleting savings due to medical expenses. Access to comprehensive care supports your wellbeing and strengthens your financial foundation.

8. **Plan Your Estate and Secure Your Legacy**
   Draft a valid, executable will, and consider structures like trusts for asset protection. Proper estate planning ensures your family is protected and your assets are distributed according to your wishes.

9. **Organise Essential Documents**
   Keep all important financial, legal, and insurance documents in one accessible place. Tools like Nikki Bush's *"What If File"* can help organise your affairs and reduce stress during emergencies or loss.

10. **Engage with Financial Advisers Early**
    Don't wait for a crisis. Partner with trusted financial professionals who can guide you through key decisions, from budgeting and investing to retirement

and estate planning. A proactive approach leads to better outcomes and greater confidence.

---

*"Financial planning is more than balancing budgets—it's about creating a life of wellness, freedom, and legacy.*

---

# Chapter 10: Wellness, Health, and Financial Planning

It is essential to incorporate wellness and health into financial planning because of the significant impact that health-related issues can have on personal finances. This chapter outlines ways to protect your financial future by prioritising health in your planning. Here are key reasons why health and wellness play a crucial role:

## 10.1. Impact of medical costs on financial security

Healthcare expenses, particularly from chronic illnesses, critical conditions, or sudden health crises, can lead to substantial out-of-pocket costs. By factoring health into your financial planning, you can ensure these expenses won't drain your savings or prevent you from meeting other financial goals.

## 10.2. Income protection and long-term care

Health affects your capacity to work and earn. Income protection insurance and disability coverage serve as essential tools to maintain financial stability in the event of an illness or disability that reduces or stops income. This form of risk management is vital, especially for primary earners.

Maintaining good health can extend your life expectancy, ultimately influencing the longevity of your retirement savings. Health also affects the need for long-term care, which can be costly. Taking health into account in your financial plan helps you prepare for these potential future expenses.

## 10.3. Preventive health and insurance savings

A commitment to wellness and preventive health can be financially rewarding as well. Healthy lifestyles often lead to lower life and health insurance premiums. Many insurers provide discounts or rewards for actions such as regular exercise, maintaining a healthy weight, and avoiding smoking.

## 10.4 Mental wellbeing and financial stress

Financial stress can negatively impact your physical health. Planning ahead by ensuring financial security can help mitigate stress, foster better mental and emotional wellbeing, and create a healthier, more resilient state of being. Health-conscious financial planning ensures timely access to healthcare resources and prepares you for future healthcare needs, including retirement healthcare funds, savings for chronic illnesses, and provisions for specialised treatments. This preparedness allows for better control over both health outcomes and financial security.

## 10.5 Healthcare preparedness: Know your health status

Staying informed about your health status (e.g. cholesterol, blood pressure, and blood sugar levels, and lifestyle factors influencing medical loadings) can help guide decisions on insurance premiums and coverage options. Some insurers offer standard rates and benefits for those maintaining healthy lifestyle habits, highlighting the importance of proactive health management in financial planning.

## *Incorporating health and wellness is essential to financial security*

- Health issues—chronic illness, sudden emergencies, or long-term care—have **direct financial consequences**.
- A truly effective financial plan must account for:
  - o **Medical costs** and out-of-pocket expenses
  - o **Income protection** in case of disability or illness
  - o **Long-term care planning**, especially as life expectancy increases
  - o **Preventive health** can reduce insurance premiums and long-term expenses

## *Wellness and mental health are financial factors too*

- Financial stress significantly impacts mental and physical wellbeing.
- Secure financial planning **reduces anxiety**, builds resilience, and supports overall life satisfaction.
- Knowing your health status can help you optimise insurance options and avoid costly premiums.

## *A new mindset and practical action are both required*

- Women must:
    - o Educate themselves on rights, planning tools, and financial strategies.
    - o Challenge outdated assumptions and take ownership of wealth building.
    - o Create safety nets through emergency funds, insurance, and estate planning.
    - o Plan with both health and financial longevity in mind.

# PART IV: TOWARDS A CULTURE OF EMPOWERMENT

## Chapter 11: Fostering Financial Literacy and Independence for Individual and Societal Impact

The journey toward financial independence is not only a personal milestone for women—it is also a societal imperative. Given the historical context and the ongoing challenges surrounding financial literacy and economic participation, especially among women, it is essential to develop targeted strategies that address both the **individual empowerment** of women and the **broader economic and social benefits** of their full financial inclusion.

This chapter explores **practical steps and interventions** that can improve women's financial literacy, encourage confident financial decision making, and create enabling environments—at home, in communities, and in the financial sector—that support sustained independence. By equipping women with the tools and knowledge to manage their finances proactively, we help build more resilient households, reduce economic dependency, and contribute to the overall growth and stability of society.

## 11.1 What can you do?

### *Practical steps for individuals*

- **Attend workshops and seminars:** Look for local events or webinars focused on financial education. By following these steps, women can build a strong financial foundation and work towards achieving financial independence. It's important to remember that financial empowerment is a journey, not a destination. These sessions can be combined with discussions about the benefits of treating spouses as partners in the marriage, which was ranked 1st place to get women into action.

- **Build a trusted relationship:** Find a financial adviser you trust and who respects your need for clarity and understanding.

- **Embrace technology:** Leverage financial applications and tools.

- **Improve financial literacy, educate yourself by reading books and articles:** Numerous resources are available that can help you understand the basics of personal finance, investing, and retirement planning.

- **Take online courses:**

    - **Coursera** (www.coursera.org) and **Udemy** (www.udemy.com): Both platforms offer a range of courses from international institutions, including some universities and instructors in

South Africa. However, the course content is generally created to be universally applicable, unless a course specifically covers South African law or finance.

- o **Khan Academy** (www.khanacademy.org): Primarily offers foundational courses, particularly in mathematics, science, and humanities, but does have financial literacy courses. It is generally aligned with the US educational curriculum and does not tailor its courses to the South African legislation or curriculum.
- o **Alison** (www.alison.com): Similar to the others, Alison provides general courses on a wide variety of topics and is internationally focused, while some courses may cover regional topics, including some applicable to South Africa.

For anyone in South Africa looking for educational resources that specifically align with South African legislation, policies, or regulations, local platforms like the University of Cape Town's online courses (in partnership with GetSmarter; www.getsmarter.com), or institutions like Unisa (www.unisa.ac.za) and Wits University (www.wits.ac.za) offer courses that may be more region-specific. Additionally, the Banking Association South Africa and South African Institute of Financial Markets may provide more localised finance-related resources tailored to South African law and policies.

## Building a legacy: Empowering the next generation

One of the key findings in our research is that women, especially those under the age of 45, more than previous generations, are beginning to prioritise financial independence. Younger women in our study ranked 'educate oneself' and 'treating spouses as equal partners' as their top priorities, reflecting a shift towards more proactive financial management. Teaching children about the importance of financial literacy and involving them in financial discussions, even around the dinner table, can set them on the path to a secure financial future.

Figure 11.1 illustrates some activities for exposing children to financial literacy.

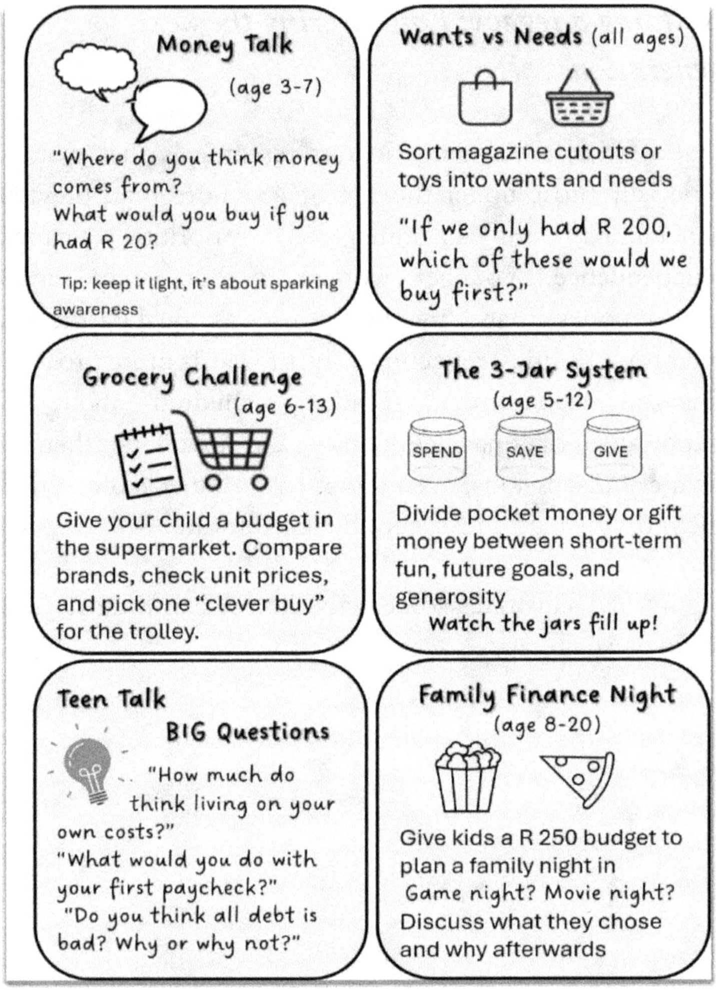

## Money Talk
(age 3-7)

"Where do you think money comes from?
What would you buy if you had R 20?

Tip: keep it light, it's about sparking awareness

## Wants vs Needs (all ages)

Sort magazine cutouts or toys into wants and needs

"If we only had R 200, which of these would we buy first?"

## Grocery Challenge
(age 6-13)

Give your child a budget in the supermarket. Compare brands, check unit prices, and pick one "clever buy" for the trolley.

## The 3-Jar System
(age 5-12)

SPEND   SAVE   GIVE

Divide pocket money or gift money between short-term fun, future goals, and generosity
Watch the jars fill up!

## Teen Talk
### BIG Questions

"How much do think living on your own costs?"
"What would you do with your first paycheck?"
"Do you think all debt is bad? Why or why not?"

## Family Finance Night
(age 8-20)

Give kids a R 250 budget to plan a family night in
Game night? Movie night?
Discuss what they chose and why afterwards

*Figure 11.1 Child-friendly activities for teaching financial literacy*

**CALL-OUT BOX 1:** *Money Talk –*
*Preschool to Early Primary School*

_____

**Let's Talk About It!** *(Ages 3–7)*
Use these simple questions at the dinner table, in the car,
or while playing. **Ask:**

- *'What do you think money is for?'*
- *'Where do you think money comes from?'*
- *'What would you buy if you had R20?'*
- *'Can you think of something you would wait to buy later?'*

**Tip:** Keep the tone light! At this age, it's about sparking
awareness, not teaching budgets.

_____

**CALL-OUT BOX 2:** *Everyday activity –*
*sorting game*

_____

**Mini-activity: Wants vs. needs game** *(all ages – customise*
*to their level)*
Grab some magazines or toys and ask your child:

*'Is this something we need to live, or something that's just nice to*
*have?'*
Create two piles: **Needs** and **Wants.**
**Ask:** *'If we only had R200, which of these would we buy first?'*

157

This helps kids distinguish between essentials and extras — a key money skill!

---

*CALL-OUT BOX 3:* *Real-life lesson — grocery edition*

---

**Grocery shop budget challenge** *(ages 6–13)*
Next time you're shopping together, try this:

Provide a budget amount so that they can make clever money choices.

**Ask:** *Let's pick a breakfast cereal and other essentials. Compare brands; which one costs less?*
Write down prices and compare brands.
Use a calculator or phone to compare unit prices.

**Bonus:** Let them choose one 'clever buy' to add to the trolley!

---

*CALL-OUT BOX 4:* *Simple saving system*

---

**The 3-Jar system** *(Ages 5–12)*
Label three jars: **Spend**, **Save**, and **Give**.

Every time your child receives money (pocket money, birthday, or for chores):

- Put some in **Spend** for short-term fun
- Some in **Save** for a future goal
- And a little in **Give** for a cause or gift

Seeing the jars fill up gives children a visual and emotional connection to their choices.

---

### *CALL-OUT BOX 5*: *Thought-provoking teen talk*

---

**Big questions for big thinkers** *(ages 13–18)*
Use these to spark deeper financial thinking with teens:

- *'What would you do with your first paycheck?'*
- *'Would you rather work for money or invest to make your money work for you?'*
- *'How much do you think living on your own costs?'*
- *'Do you think all debt is bad? Why or why not?'*

These questions open doors to powerful values conversations.

---

CALL-OUT BOX 6: *Family finance*
*night*

---

**Activity: Plan a family fun night – on a budget!** *(ages 8–teen)*

Give your kids a R250 'budget' to plan a night:

- Will it be movie snacks and Netflix/BoxOffice?
- A homemade pizza party?
- Game night with a homemade prize.

Then ask: *'How did you decide what to spend on? Was it hard to choose?'*

This builds planning, prioritisation, and real-world application skills.

## 11.2. What should society be doing?

### *Developing and sustaining financial literacy programmes and supportive networks*

Financial literacy programmes should be designed to address the specific needs and circumstances of women. These programmes can include workshops, online courses, and community-based initiatives that provide practical financial education specifically focused on women. Key areas of focus should include budgeting, saving, investing, retirement planning, and understanding financial products and services. Women can benefit from supportive networks that provide mentorship, guidance, and encouragement. Financial institutions, non-profits, and community organisations can facilitate the creation of these networks, offering women a platform to share experiences, seek advice, and learn from one another.

## Leveraging technology for financial empowerment

Technology can play a significant role in enhancing financial literacy. Mobile apps, online platforms, and social media can provide accessible and engaging financial education resources. These tools can also offer personalised financial planning assistance, helping women to make informed decisions and track their financial progress. The Financial Planning Institute of Southern Africa (https://fpi.co.za/) and provider companies can provide specific tools to assist women with their unique financial planning needs.

## Promoting gender equality in the workplace

Employers have a critical role in promoting gender equality and supporting women's financial empowerment. This includes implementing fair pay practices, offering flexible work arrangements, and providing opportunities for career advancement.

By creating an inclusive workplace culture, employers can help women achieve financial independence and stability.

## *Encouraging policy reforms*

Advocating for policy reforms that address gender disparities in financial literacy and economic participation is essential. This includes pushing for changes in tax laws, pension regulations, and employment policies that disadvantage women. Policymakers should consider the unique challenges faced by women and develop legislation that promotes financial equality and empowerment.

## 11.3 Key takeaways

**Financial independence is both personal and societal:** Empowering women financially strengthens not only individuals and households but also the broader economy and social fabric.

**Education is the foundation of empowerment:** Building financial literacy through books, online courses, and workshops is critical for enabling informed financial decisions.

**Start early, teach financial literacy to children:** Age-appropriate tools like games, dinner-table questions, and budgeting challenges help children develop healthy financial habits from an early age.

**Build trust with financial advisers:** Women should seek out trusted financial professionals who respect their need for clarity, partnership, and long-term support.

**Leverage technology for learning and management:** Mobile apps, online platforms, and financial tools provide accessible, personalised ways to track progress and make smarter decisions.

**Younger generations are leading the shift:** Women under 45 are prioritising financial independence and treating spouses as equal financial partners, setting a powerful example for the future.

**Supportive networks and mentorship matter:** Peer support, community initiatives, and mentorship programmes help women build confidence, share knowledge, and stay accountable.

**Employers have a role to play:** Companies should promote gender equity by ensuring fair pay, flexible work arrangements, and professional growth opportunities.

**Policy reform is essential:** Legislative changes must address gender-specific economic challenges and promote financial equality, especially in tax, pension, and employment systems.

**Financial empowerment is a lifelong journey:** It's not a one-time event. It requires ongoing learning, intentional planning, and support from individuals, institutions, and society as a whole.

---

*When women are financially empowered, the ripple effects transform families, workplaces, and entire economies.*

---

# Chapter 12: The Cost of Staying— Why Women Remain in Unhealthy Relationships

It's a question often asked, sometimes with judgement:
**'Why doesn't she just leave?'**

But the answer is rarely simple and often rooted in **money**.

For many women, financial dependence is the invisible chain that keeps them bound to relationships that no longer serve their wellbeing emotionally, mentally, or even physically. The fear of not being able to support themselves or, worse, their children, can outweigh the fear of staying. Survival can feel more attainable than freedom when you've been conditioned to believe that you are not capable, qualified, or entitled to stand on your own.

## 12.1 It's not just emotional. It's economic.

Behind the silence of many women are very real and pressing questions:

- *Where would I live?*
- *How would I afford rent, food, school fees, transport?*
- *Who would hire me at this age?*
- *What if I can't make it alone?*

These are not signs of weakness; they're signs of systemic financial exclusion. Generational messages have told women to be 'grateful for stability,' even when it comes at the cost of peace. Many have never been taught how to manage money, budget independently, or build assets in their own name. Some were discouraged from working, investing, or even asking questions about household finances.

**And so, they stay.**

## 12.2 The cultural and spiritual weight

In some communities, the pressure to maintain the image of a 'perfect family' is immense. Women are expected to endure, to forgive endlessly, to sacrifice. Spiritual teachings, while meant to uplift, have sometimes been misused to justify suffering, telling women to pray through trauma instead of acting on their God-given wisdom and strength.

## 12.3 Freedom begins with a financial plan

Empowerment doesn't start the day a woman walks out the door. It starts **long before** that with a bank account in her name, a written budget, basic knowledge of her rights, a support network, and the quiet rebuilding of confidence.

This book exists to be part of that foundation because no woman should have to choose between safety and survival.

**Emergency financial planning – When you're preparing to leave an unhealthy relationship**

Leaving an unsafe or controlling environment often requires discreet, strategic preparation. These steps are designed for those who may be experiencing financial control, emotional manipulation, or domestic abuse.

**Step-by-step financial safety planning**

1.  **Open a secret, independent bank account**
   *   Use a trusted friend's address or a PO box, if needed.
   *   Consider an online-only bank for discretion.
2.  **Gather important documents (and copies)**
   *   Driver's license, passport, ID card
   *   Birth certificates (for you and your children)
   *   Medical and financial records
   *   Hide or store them securely — with a friend, lawyer, or in the cloud.

3.  **Stash emergency cash slowly and secretly**
   *   Small amounts over time — R100 or R200 bills hidden in safe places
   *   Consider loading prepaid debit cards if you can't carry cash

### 4. Create a list of trusted contacts

- Friends, coworkers, counsellors, shelters
- Memorize at least two phone numbers in case you lose your phone
- Secure your digital identity
  1. Set up new email accounts and passwords
  2. Use private browsing, especially when researching help or finances
  3. Turn off shared family accounts on mobile devices (location sharing, cloud photos, etc.)

### 5. Develop a safety exit plan

- Know where you'll go — even temporarily
- Pack a 'go bag' with essentials: clothes, documents, medications, cash, keys, kids' comfort items

When a woman owns her financial future, she reclaims her voice. She begins to dream again. She no longer negotiates her worth.

You don't have to have it all figured out today. But **starting quietly, confidently, and deliberately** is the beginning of freedom. You are not alone. And you are stronger than you've been told.

If you or someone you know is in an unsafe relationship, or if financial abuse or control may be part of the situation, **refer to the Appendix** for national resources that offer legal, emotional, financial, and emergency support.

## 12.4 Key takeaways

**Financial dependence is a primary barrier:** Many women stay in unhealthy relationships because of economic insecurity—fear of having no housing, food, funds for school fees, or unemployment often outweighs the fear of abuse.

**Systemic and generational exclusion shapes choices:** Cultural norms, lack of financial literacy, and discouragement from managing money or working have left many women without assets or independent financial security.

**Cultural and spiritual pressures reinforce staying:** Societal expectations of 'perfect families' and misapplied spiritual teachings often pressure women to endure suffering rather than seek safety and independence.

**Freedom begins with financial preparation:** Empowerment starts before leaving. Opening a personal bank account, budgeting, learning legal rights, and building confidence and support networks are crucial steps.

**Emergency financial planning is a lifeline:** Practical strategies—such as discreetly saving cash, gathering documents, securing digital identity, and preparing a safety exit plan—help women leave unsafe environments with greater security.

# PART V: FINAL REFLECTIONS AND FUTURE DIRECTIONS

## Chapter 13: Final Thoughts on Financial Empowerment

As we've explored throughout this book, financial empowerment is not just about understanding numbers; it's about **transforming your relationship with money.** From the data collected in our study, we see a clear divide between how women and men approach financial planning. Many women in the sample only began planning for retirement when it was mandatory, such as through employer-sponsored retirement funds. Furthermore, the use of professional services like tax consultants and financial advisers was significantly lower among women than among men. This gap is an opportunity for you to take charge and make informed decisions about your financial future. Reach out to me today to put you in touch with a financial adviser to address your needs!

As we conclude this journey into financial empowerment, it's important to reflect on the insights gained from our study. The data clearly indicates that while women are becoming more aware of the need for financial independence, there is still a significant gap in financial literacy and proactive planning. This book has provided you with the insight and knowledge to bridge that gap, **but the responsibility to take action lies with you.**

**It is a multifaceted challenge that requires concerted efforts from individuals, institutions, and policymakers.** By addressing the systemic barriers and providing targeted support, we can create a more equitable and prosperous society where women are fully empowered to take control of their financial futures.

**Whether it's starting with small steps like creating a budget or making the bold move to consult with a financial adviser,** every action you take brings you closer to financial empowerment. Remember, it's not just about planning for retirement—it's about ensuring that you're prepared for any eventuality, that you understand your financial rights, and that you're confident in the decisions you make.

The most important takeaway is to **show up for yourself.** Financial empowerment is about taking control of your life and your future. The time to start is now!

## 13.1 What's next?

The data collected during the study discussed in this book were not representative of South Africa's population. Studies involving other financial companies, industries, cities, and countries with similar variables are necessary, as findings were not generalisable across the population of South Africa.

Future interventions should also focus on expanding the behavioural attitude of women, as some of the *in vivo* quotes to justify reasons for not involving women in finance were: 'my wife knows how to *spend* money, but not how to *make* money', 'the credit card has a limit, it is not a target', 'finance is a man's job, let me deal with it'.

Understanding why men and women view financial advisory services as an individual matter, focused only on the breadwinner, rather than on both partners, would also be insightful. This phenomenon may be the result of a lack of trust in the relationship, not wanting to disclose too much financial information to remain in control, not trusting that they will remain married or for psychological reasons. They may also not understand how advisers are being remunerated and therefore don't want to make *unnecessary* calls that might not be of benefit to them.

Women in our study ranked *'educated at home'* as one of the top reasons for moving women to action.

The development of **financial education programmes** that can be launched **at the high school level** should also be prioritised. Introducing compulsory financial education at the secondary school level could be a game-changer for long-term financial wellbeing and empowerment, especially in a country where youth unemployment and intergenerational poverty remain serious challenges.

In **South Africa**, financial literacy rates remain low, particularly among youth, contributing to debt cycles, dependency, and vulnerability to financial abuse. Many young adults enter adulthood without understanding credit, contracts, marriage regimes, or even how to open a bank account. The long-term impact? Poor financial choices, legal entanglements, and missed opportunities for wealth building. To create a well-rounded **financial education** programme, curriculum content should be **practical, locally relevant, and progressive by grade level. At the high school level, it** can be structured around three key themes:

## 1. Basic financial literacy (Grades 8–9)

- Understanding money: income, spending, saving
- Bank accounts: how to open and manage them
- Cash vs. digital banking (eWallets, mobile money)
- Budgeting skills: weekly, monthly, and event-based
- Understanding interest (simple vs. compound)

## 2. Life skills: legal and financial responsibilities (Grades 10–11)

- **Marriage regimes** in South Africa:
    - In community of property vs out of community (with or without accrual)
    - Legal implications of marriage and divorce on assets
- Rental contracts, credit agreements, and cell phone contracts

- Basic tax concepts (what is SARS, how PAYE works)
- Saving vs. investing (accessibility, risk, goals)

### 3. Advanced practical application (Grade 12)
- Long-term financial planning:
  - Retirement, emergency funds, debt management
- Career planning and income forecasting
- Entrepreneurship basics and business budgeting
- Scams and financial fraud awareness
- Accessing independent financial advice (e.g. avoiding biased sales reps or pyramid schemes)

Several countries have implemented strong financial literacy programmes that South Africa can draw inspiration from. **Australia's MoneySmart Teaching Program** is integrated across subjects (math, economics, life orientation), offers free tools, case studies, and lesson plans for teachers, and emphasises real-world decision making and family financial responsibilities. In **Sweden, personal finance is included in the social science curriculum** from the age of 13, and focuses on ethical consumption, sustainability, and budgeting. Financial literacy rates are high among Swedish youth. In the **US**, a **full semester personal finance course** is a requirement in some states **(e.g. Utah, Missouri).** Courses cover credit, savings, taxes, insurance, and even investing. Students also undergo real-life simulations, where they are required to 'live' a month on a mock income. In Kenya, Afloutan International (together with its local partners) has implemented financial education embedded in life skills programmes. The programmes focus on child rights, saving, budgeting, and small-scale entrepreneurship and are adaptable to rural and low-resource contexts. However, before launching a national curriculum in South Africa, the following areas need attention:

- **Curriculum alignment** with the CAPS and life orientation.
- **Teacher training**: Educators may need upskilling in financial concepts.
- **Public–private partnerships**: Banks, NGOs, and financial technology firms could provide support in the form of funding, resources, and experiential learning.
- **Digital access and equity**: Students in under-resourced schools must be able to access materials and simulations.
- **Monitoring and evaluation**: What impact does financial education have on students' behaviour 1, 3, and 5 years after grade 12?

---

*Teaching a teenager how to budget, understand marital contracts, and open a bank account is as important as teaching them algebra or Shakespeare. It empowers them to make informed, independent choices for life.*

---

## 13.2 Conclusion

Determining the exact loss to the economy associated with women not fully participating in financial decision making may prioritise further research by policymakers to increase the fiduciary responsibilities of financial service professionals. This determination will assist women in understanding their financial position at specific eventualities, i.e. death and divorce, based on their marriage regimes, timeously. The *'fiduciary responsibility'* of financial service professionals was ranked by women in the focus groups as one of the top five priorities to move women to action.

The need for *'being looked after'* and that of *'being feminine'* may also be explored in more detail to understand the influence of power, religion, and culture on women's financial decision making. There are many international studies which discuss the financial implications of women's disempowerment for their economies. In contrast, few South African studies examine this issue in depth. Those who do tend to focus on employment equity only, without addressing women's financial literacy or the impact this has on their retirement.

### The time is now

For too long, too many women have allowed external voices—partners, family expectations, cultural traditions, or even fear itself—to shape their relationship with money.

But the world has changed. The laws have changed. And so must we.

Legislation like FICA has made it clear: your financial identity must be in your own name. Your power must be your own too. You don't need to be an economist to take charge. You don't need permission to plan. You don't have to wait for tragedy or transition to realise that the best security is self-agency. When women take control of their money, they take control of their choices. They speak differently. They negotiate better. They sleep with less fear and walk with more purpose. They change the story not just for themselves but for their children and the generations that follow.

This book was never just about bank accounts or legal documents. It's about wholeness. Freedom. Knowing your worth and backing it up with informed, intentional action. So don't wait for perfect. Start where you are, with what you have—and build. You owe that to yourself. Because financial independence isn't a privilege, it's your right. And it's your responsibility.

## Want More Tools to Start Your Journey and to Start Talking to Your Children About Money?

You've just taken a powerful step toward creating financial confidence in your family. Now let's keep going—together.

**Join me online at** *https://estellepieterse.co.za* **you'll find:**

- **free downloads:** Printable **money conversation cards**, budget worksheets, and starter kits.
- **monthly money notes:** Real-talk tips, quick wins, and stories to inspire you.
- **webinars and workshops:** Learn how to teach children about money, navigate your own financial path, and build confidence.
- **budget template** to download.
- **coaching:** Want to bring this message to your school, company, or community?

Scan the QR code to download your free Family Money Starter Kit and other content and Tools or to Book a Session.

*Scan me!*

# ABBREVIATIONS

| | |
|---|---|
| ANC | Antenuptial contract |
| CAPS | Curriculum and Assessment Policy Statement |
| DC | Defined contribution (pension plans) |
| DB | Defined benefit (pension plans) |
| FAIS | Financial Advisory and Intermediary Services (Act) |
| FICA | Financial Intelligence Centre Act |
| FSCA | Financial Sector Conduct Authority |
| JSE | Johannesburg Stock Exchange |
| PAYE | Pay as you earn |
| SARS | South African Revenue Service |
| | Stats SA Statistics South Africa |
| UNESCO | United Nations Educational, Scientific, and Cultural Organization |
| UK | United Kingdom |
| US | United States of America |

# BIBLIOGRAPHY

Alessie, R., Van Rooij, M., & Lusardi, A. (2011). Financial literacy and retirement preparation in the Netherlands. *Journal of Pension Economics and Finance,* 10(4), 527-545.

American Association of University Women Educational Foundation (2007). Behind the pay gap. Available from www.aauw.org

American Association of University Women (2012). Graduating to a pay gap. Available from www.aauw.org/files/2013/02/graduating-to-a-pay-gap-the-earnings-of-women-and-men-one-year-after-college-graduation.pdf [Accessed 21 October 2017].

Aronson, J. (1994). A pragmatic view of thematic analysis. *Qualitative Report,* 2(1).

Atkinson, P., & Delamont, S. (eds) (2010). *SAGE qualitative research methods.* Thousand Oaks, CA: SAGE Publications.

Babcock, L., & Laschever, S. (2008). *Ask for it: How Women Can Use the Power of Negotiation to get What They Really Want.* New York: Bantam Dell.

Barter, C., & Renold, E. (1999). The use of vignettes in qualitative research. *Social Research Update,* 25.

Bartunek, J. M., & Murnighan, J. K. (1984). The nominal group technique: Expanding the basic procedure and underlying assumptions. *Group and Organization Studies,* 9, 417-432.

Batliwala, S. (1994). The meaning of women's empowerment: New concepts from action. In. Sen, G., Germain, A., & Chen, L. C. (eds) *Population Policies Reconsidered: Health, Empowerment, and Rights.* Boston: Harvard School of Public Health.

Bosch, A. (2017). Rethinking women's workplace outcomes: Structural inequality. In Bosch, A. (ed.) *South African Board for People Practices Women's Report 2017,* pp. 13-17. Rosebank, South Africa: SABPP.

Bush, N. (2019). What If file for when a *What If* moment strikes. Available from: https://nikkibush.com/what-if-file-for-when-a-what-if-moment-strikes [Accessed 22 March 2025].

Charmaz, K. (2000). Grounded theory: Objectivist and constructivist methods. In: Denzin, N.K. & Lincoln, Y. S. *Strategies for Qualitative Inquiry.* Thousand Oaks, Ca: SAGE Publications

Choi, J. J., David, L., & Madrian, B. C. (2004). Plan design and 401(k) savings outcomes. *National Tax Journal* 57(2), 1, 275-298.

Collins, J. M. (2011). Improving financial literacy: The role of non-profit providers. In: Mitchell, O. S. & Lusardi, A. (eds) *Financial Literacy: Implications for Retirement Security and the Financial Marketplace.* Oxford: Oxford University Press, 268-287.

Corbin, J., & Strauss, A. (2016). Basics of Qualitative
Research: Techniques and Procedures for Developing
Grounded Theory. Thousand Oaks, Ca: SAGE
Publications.

Delbecq, A. L., & Van de Ven, A. H. (1971). A group
process model for problem identification and program
planning. *Journal of Applied Behavioral Science*, 7, 466-491.

Demirgüç-Kunt, A., Klapper, L., & Singer, D. (2013).
*Financial inclusion and legal discrimination against women: Evidence
from developing countries* (Policy Research Working Paper No.
6416). The World Bank. https://doi.org/10.1596/1813-
9450-6416

Duflo, E., & Saez, E. (2004). The role of information and
social interactions in retirement plan decisions: Evidence
from a randomized experiment. *The Quarterly Journal of
Economics*, 118(3), 815-842.

Finch, J. (1987). The vignette technique in survey research.
*Sociology*, 21, 105-114.

Finke, M. S. (2013). Financial advice: Does it make a
difference? In: Mitchell, O. S. & Smetters, K. (eds) *The
market for retirement financial advice*. 229-248. Oxford: Oxford
University Press.

First Person Consulting Pty Ltd (n.d.). *Introduction to
Qualitative Data Analysis*. Australia: First Person Consulting.
Available from
www.fpconsulting.com.au/uploads/2/4/9/6/24962042/q
ualitative_analysis_guide.pdf [Accessed 30 November

2017].

**Human Sciences Research Council.** (1986). *The effect of joint taxation on the participation of married women in the labour force.* Pretoria: HSRC

Hung, A., Yoong, J., & Brown, E. (2012). Empowering women through financial awareness and education. *OECD Working Papers on Finance, Insurance and Private Pensions, No. 14,* Organisation for Economic Co-operation and Development. Available from http://dx.doi.org/10.1787/5k9d5v6kh56g-en [Accessed 21 October 2017].

Kunene, M. (2025). **Later vows, sooner splits: South Africans marrying older as divorce rates climb. Caxton Network News. Available from** https://www.citizen.co.za/network-news/lnn/article/later-vows-sooner-splits-south-africans-marrying-older-as-divorce-rates-climb/#:~:text=According%20to%20Stats%20SA%2C%2022%20230%20divorces%20were,couples%20whose%20unions%20lasted%20less%20than%2010%20years. [Accessed 17 May 2025].

Lewis-Beck, M., Bryman, A., & Liao, T. F. (2004). The SAGE Encyclopedia of Social Science Research Methods. Thousand Oaks, Ca: SAGE Publications.

Lusardi, A., & Mitchell, O. S. (2014). The economic importance of financial literacy: Theory and evidence. *Journal of Economic Literature,* 52(1), 5-44.

**Margo Commission.** (1986). *Report of the Commission of Inquiry into the Tax Structure of the Republic of South Africa* (RP34/1987). Pretoria: Government Printer.

McKeen, C. A., & Bujaki, M. (1994). Women's experiences in the accounting profession: A literature review. *Canadian Woman Studies, 14*(3), 30–34.

**Mertens, D. M. (2009).** *Transformative Research and Evaluation.* Guilford Press.Miles, M. B., & Huberman, A. M. (1994). *Qualitative data analysis: An expanded sourcebook.* London: SAGE Publications.

Miller, R., & Brewer, J. (2003). *The A-Z of social research: A dictionary of key social science research concepts.* London: SAGE Publications.

Old Mutual, Legal Services, South Africa, and the Commission of Inquiry into the Tax Structure of the Republic of South Africa. (1987). The Margo Commission's Report Into the Tax Structure of South Africa: An Overview. Old Mutual.

Pieterse, E. (2017). The attitude of women towards financial planning. Final Research Assignment. University of Stellenbosch, South Africa.

Preller, B. (n.d.) *Divorce in South Africa: A Comprehensive Graphical Comparison of the 2022 Divorce Statistics.* Family Laws South Africa. Available from: https://familylaws.co.za/divorce-statistics-south-africa-released-2024/ [Accessed 19 October 2022].

Rowley, J. (2012). Conducting research interviews. *Management Research Review*, 34 (3/4),260-271.

Segar, J., & White, A. (1992). *Gender, power, and financial literacy: A critical perspective on economic education for women.* Journal of Economic Issues, 26(2), 473–481.

SST Attorneys. (2020). Marital regimes in South Africa – How should i get married? Available from https://www.sstlaw.co.za/uncategorized/marital-regimes-in-south-africa-how-should-i-get-married/[Accessed 19 October 2024].

Statistics South Africa. (2023). *Mid-year population estimates 2023* (Statistical Release P0302). Pretoria: Stats SA. Retrieved from https://www.statssa.gov.za/publications/P0302/P030220 23.pdfUNESCO Global Education Monitoring Report Team. (2020). Global Education Monitoring Report 2020: Gender Report, A new generation: 25 years of efforts for gender equality in education. Paris: UNESCO

Vendros, K. R. (1979). The nominal group technique is a participatory, planning method in adult education. Ph.D. dissertation, Florida State University, Tallahassee.

Willis, L. E. (2011). The financial education fallacy. *American Economic Review*, 101(3), 429-434.

Yin, R. K. (2003). *Case study research: Design and methods* (3rd ed.). Applied Social Research Methods Series Volume 5. Thousand Oaks, CA: SAGE Publications.

Young, T. (2020). Why Elvis Presley was censored on The Ed Sullivan Show. Elvis Presley biography. Available from https://elvisbiography.net/2020/09/09/why-elvis-presley-was-censored-on-the-ed-sullivan-show/ [Accessed 09 October 2025].

Zikmund, W. G., Babin, B. J., Carr, J. C., & Griffin, M. (2013). *Business research methods* (9th ed.). South-Western USA: Cengage Learning.

# APPENDIX: EMERGENCY AND CRISIS RESOURCES

## Emergency and crisis helplines

Gender-based Violence Command Centre (24/7 support)
– National Helpline

📞 0800 428 428

📱 Dial 1207867# from a cell phone to request a call back

✉ support@genderbasedviolence.org.za

🔗 www.gbv.org.za

Lifeline South Africa
Offers trauma counselling, emotional support, and crisis intervention

📞 0861 322 322

🔗 www.lifeline.org.za

People Opposing Women Abuse (POWA)
Offers shelter, legal advice, counselling, and advocacy

📞 011 642 4345 / 6

🔗 www.powa.co.za

## Legal and financial support

Legal Aid South Africa
Free legal advice and representation to qualifying individuals

📞 0800 110 110 | SMS 'Legal' to 079 835 7179

🔗 www.legal-aid.co.za

Black Sash
Advocacy for social justice, grants access, and legal

empowerment

☎ 072 66 33 739

🔗 www.blacksash.org.za

## Shelters and safe houses

TEARS Foundation
National database of safe houses and gender-based
violence support services

📱 SMS 'Help' to 1347355# (free USSD service)

🔗 www.tears.co.za

Saartjie Baartman Centre for Women and Children
(Western Cape)
Shelter, counselling, job readiness programmes

☎ 021 633 5287 / 021 633 5287 (24hr line)

🔗 www.saartjiebaartmancentre.org.za

## Digital and emotional safety

- Use private browsing or **incognito mode** when
  accessing help.
- Log out of shared accounts and turn off **location
  tracking** on mobile devices.
- Avoid using shared devices to search for support.

**Advance Praise for** *Change Your Perspective, Change Your Life!*

"It is imperative that every woman is educated and empowered to manage her finances, and Estelle's book contributes to achieving this goal."
— Jeanette Marais, CEO of Momentum Group

"It provides practical examples and stories, which the reader can relate to—making her points and practical suggestions easier to understand."
— Jennifer van Oerle, COO of Invest, Discovery Group

"When a woman controls her finances, she controls her future."
— Nikki Bush, award-winning speaker and author of *Future-proof Yourself*

www.ingramcontent.com/pod-product-compliance
Lightning Source LLC
Chambersburg PA
CBHW060850280326
41934CB00007B/994